LONDON MISSION:
THE FIRST CRITICAL YEARS

LONDON MISSION:
THE FIRST
CRITICAL
YEARS

By Jack L. Cross

MICHIGAN STATE
UNIVERSITY PRESS 1968

★
★
★
★
★

Manufactured in the United States of America

For Geoffrey whose promise I hope to keep,
and for Dorothy and Gregory who will help
me to keep it.

Contents

Introduction

Diplomacy is an art not a science. Thomas Pinckney, an artful diplomat, wallows in obscurity—partially as the result of the partisanship that destroyed the political consensus of the Washington Administration and, in part, because of the judgments passed on Pinckney and his mission by later historians. The generalizations about him and his work stem from scholarship originating in the 1920's. They have become part of the traditional version of our early history. This book is an attempt to modify those generalizations and to reassess Pinckney's role in the light of the full documentary background of his mission.

In the course of my research, I have become fascinated by the man, as elusive an individual as one is likely to find. There was a formality and stiffness about him that prevents us from ever knowing him as a human being. Only the most daring writer would essay a biography of him on the basis of the documentary evidence he left behind. He appears to have been restrained, cold, and humorless.

But for all that his services to the nation were great, and in these accomplishments revisited in detailed analysis, his reputation may find its place among those of a generation of venerable men.

How significant a contribution this work may be, I leave to

my peers. If it corrects in some small measure some historical interpretations of this period of our history, then I will have accomplished my purpose.

In writing this book I have become indebted to a number of people. To William T. Hutchinson and Walter Johnson, gentlemen and scholars both, my thanks. To the reference staff of the Manuscripts Division of the Library of Congress, to the staff at the National Archives and to all others in the various libraries visited, my deepest appreciation. I am especially indebted to the staffs of the South Carolina Historical Society and the Charlestown Library and Museum. The courtesies extended to me by the curators of the manuscript collections of the New York State Historical Society and of Columbia University are gratefully acknowledged.

Friends and critics have given me valuable counsel. Samuel Flagg Bemis read the manuscript and generously gave me advice. Mario Rodríguez offered me detailed criticism from which the work has profited immensely, and Elizabeth Shaw helped me to edit the manuscript.

A book doesn't come to be without the patient and wise guidance of a publisher. I have no adequate words with which to thank Lyle Blair and Jean Busfield of the Michigan State University Press for their support and interest in the publication of this work. Whatever faults remain are entirely mine.

Jack L. Cross

Austin, Texas, 1968

A Surprise Appointment

I

*Enclosed is the letter to Majr. Pinckney. For the reason's (sic) men-
tioned to you yesterday, I prefer London to Paris for his Mission.*

—Washington to Jefferson, 9 November 1791

WHEN GREAT BRITAIN and the United States decided to
exchange ministers plenipotentiary in 1791—the first
formal exchange under the Constitution—George Washington
selected South Carolinian Thomas Pinckney to represent American interests at the Court of St. James. Pinckney's appointment caused surprise and consternation. Secretary of State
Jefferson wrote to his former secretary, William Short, in
cypher, that he was totally unprepared for the nomination.[1]
The New England group expected John Adams to receive
the appointment.

Who was this little-known man whose strongest if not sole
supporter appeared to be the nation's Chief Executive?

Thomas Pinckney was born on October 23, 1750, the young-
est son of Charles and Elizabeth Lucas Pinckney. Charles Pinckney was, for a short time, chief justice of the province, and
Elizabeth Lucas achieved fame for introducing indigo culture

to South Carolina. When, in 1753, Charles was appointed agent for the province, the family sailed for England. Although the father and mother returned to America in 1758, Thomas and his older brother, Charles Cotesworth, remained in England where both finished their education. Like his older brother, Thomas attended Westminster School and Oxford and studied law at the Middle Temple. He spent one year studying military tactics and fortifications at the French Royal Military Academy in Caen. Thomas returned to Charleston in 1774, was immediately admitted to the bar in South Carolina, and began to practice law. His professional activities were interrupted, however, by the American Revolution in which he fought for six years, by his two-term governorship of South Carolina, and by his missions to Great Britain as Minister Plenipotentiary and to Spain as Envoy Extraordinary.[2]

Pinckney's distinguished service during the American Revolution was continuous from 1775 to 1781. In 1780, he was wounded in the Battle of Camden, taken prisoner, and held for one year. During the war he rose to the rank of major, having served in capacities ranging from drill master and recruiter to fortification engineer and aide to Count d'Estaing. In 1781, while recruiting in Virginia, he met Lafayette and became his lifelong friend.[3] Washington was fully aware of Pinckney's service in the cause of independence. In a memorandum submitted to the Secretary of War in 1798 listing the men he considered the "most intelligent and active officers of the late American Army," Washington emphasized Thomas Pinckney's name.[4]

From 1782 until 1787 Pinckney practiced law in Charleston. In 1787 he became Governor of South Carolina and was re-elected in 1788. During his term in office the state sent delegates to the Constitutional Convention in Philadelphia. Pinckney's brother, Charles Cotesworth, and a cousin, Charles, were among the South Carolina delegates. The contributions of that delegation to the formation of the Constitution were great, although disputed in detail by Constitutional historians, and

South Carolina was among the first states to ratify the Constitution.[5]

From the beginning of his Administration, Washington had tried to get the Pinckneys to serve in the Federal Government. In 1789 Thomas refused the offer of a district judgeship.[6] In 1791 Charles Cotesworth and his relative, Rutledge, declined seats on the Federal bench because they thought they could better serve the "federal" cause of government in their own localities.[7] But with the appointment of Pinckney to the Court of St. James, Washington succeeded at last in bringing into service an influential southern Federalist, a successful planter (hence a good representative of the "agricultural interest"), a confirmed patriot of the American Revolution and an officer of the Cincinnati, and the brother of a close personal friend, Charles Cotesworth Pinckney. Although the post was to mean great personal sacrifice,[8] and Pinckney at forty-one was a little hesitant about his qualifications for such an important assignment, he was persuaded to overcome momentary misgivings and accept the appointment.[9]

The delay from 1787 to 1791 in arranging for an exchange of representatives between Great Britain and the United States can best be explained by the exigencies of the period. At the end of the American Revolution the newly freed American colonies began to devise a system of government. It was a time of trial and error, of experiment and failure. Although the young Republic was concerned about establishing itself among the nations of the world, it was primarily interested in domestic affairs, and the first few feeble efforts to attain recognition and respect from more powerful countries met with scant success. The direction of foreign affairs, like other governmental powers logically belonging to a strong executive branch, suffered neglect under the Articles of Confederation.

With the adoption of the Constitution, however, this state of affairs began to change. As Congress, following the lead of Hamilton in his famous reports on public credit, manufacturers, and a central banking system, gave strength to the new

Federal Government, the executive branch turned to the world outside, attempting to establish the nation on a sound basis by settling differences outstanding between the United States and the world powers, particularly Great Britain. Contrary to the terms of the Treaty of Paris, Britain retained possession of military posts in the Northwest, and American citizens would not pay their debts to British creditors.

While the Revolution had established American independence, the absence of a treaty regulating commercial intercourse between the two countries illustrated how far matters must proceed before real independence could be realized. During the period under the Articles of Confederation, Great Britain had been able by economic means to divide and conquer the loosely federated colonies. The absence of a strong national government and of a treaty meant that each state negotiated its own terms of trade and set its own commodity and tonnage duties. Thus, Great Britain had maintained a distinct advantage.

It was one thing for France and Spain to encourage American rebellion against British authority, but it was quite another for them to grant commercial privileges once independence was attained. In fact, in this time of mercantilism America faced commercial restrictions by all trading nations and particularly by Great Britain, France, and Spain. These restrictions were to cause several recurring crises in the years immediately ahead. A further result of the restrictions was to cut off American commerce from profitable sources of trade to which it had grown accustomed under the British flag. By 1786, however, commerce with the French, Dutch, and Danish West Indies had grown considerably, and American trade was channeled toward the British home islands, the Mediterranean, and the Far East.[10]

Meanwhile, other factors encouraged the rapid development of American trade. Following the outbreak of the French Revolution in 1789, American commerce became a pawn in the struggle between the contending European powers. Although the British from 1783 to 1790 seemed content to ignore all overtures for a lasting commercial arrangement with her former colonies, and France treated the powerless young Government with disdain, the Nootka Sound Affair in 1789 caused Britain to understand the necessity for wooing America as an active ally, and the first diplomatic feelers were extended for an exchange of representatives and a permanent arrangement for commercial interchange.

In the 1790's, the period of Pinckney's mission to London, the importance and influence of agriculture upon American affairs was great. Tench Coxe, in the first major economic treatise written in the early national period, spoke of the significance of agriculture to the founding fathers during their debates on the Constitution. In *An Enquiry into the Principles on Which a Commercial System for the United States of America Should Be Founded; to Which Are Added Some Political Observations Connected with the Subject*, published in 1787, Coxe observed that agricultural commodities comprised the vast majority of goods, by bulk and value, going out of and coming into the country. As an industry, agriculture supplied Americans with clothing, food, and materials for the growing but still infant industries, and at the same time, the products of agriculture consumed at home were four to five times greater in quantity than those shipped abroad. The labor force was nine-tenths agricultural. In fact, in those days of unsophisticated statistical analysis, it included almost the entire population.

Such economic theory as existed in America at that time was predominantly physiocratic. Jefferson, for instance, wrote Washington from Paris in 1787 that ". . . agriculture . . . is our wisest pursuit, because it will in the end contribute most to real wealth, good morals, and happiness."[11] Thus, agriculture was the source of all *good* and goods. As Coxe concluded in his pamphlet to the founding fathers, "Agriculture appears to be the spring of our commerce, and the parent of our manufactures. . . ."[12]

By 1790, according to Coxe, the American economy had en-

tered a new era. The young Republic was beginning the up-
ward curve of rapid economic growth, contrary to the speculations of Lord Sheffield whose analysis predicting a static
economy for the colonies persuaded many Englishmen that
Great Britain could and would maintain her advantage.
America's carrying trade approximated six hundred and fifty
thousand tons of cargo, and its coasting trade equaled almost
one hundred thousand tons in 1791. These ships were vict-
ualed, for the most part, by American merchants who also furnished supplies for an additional two hundred and sixty-three
thousand tons of foreign vessels trading with U.S. ports.[13]
America was gaining economic independence from the sources
of supply, not only in shipping, but also in the production of
certain commodities. In 1790 American merchants imported
over two and a half million pounds of tea directly from China,
with the result that tea was cheaper on the Philadelphia market than it was in London in November of that year. The same
year, U.S. ships imported two and a half million bushels of salt
as ballast from Portugal, France, and Spain. Although the U.S.
population was about four million in 1790, only 70,450 pairs
of shoes and boots were imported in that year, whereas over
five thousand pairs were exported. In paper, too, America became virtually self-sufficient. Substitutes for other products had
been successfully developed, i.e., grain alcohols were rapidly re-
placing rum in production and consumption, reducing America's dependence of the West Indian trade.[14] Even in the production of fine and coarse hats and in the publication of books,
America was almost independent. True, the publications were
largely pirated from European works, but freedom from British production in these and other lines meant, in plain terms,
that the United States was, in some commodities at least, "an
open market." No single nation any longer exercised a monopoly over its trade either as supplier or purchaser of goods. Finished goods, of course, continued to be supplied from Europe,
particularly England, but important strides toward economic
independence had been taken. The new prosperity appeared so

promising that Coxe foresaw tremendous benefits accruing to America if she could avoid entanglement in European conflicts.[15] Although he may have exaggerated the degree of American independence from European and particularly British workshops, Coxe was optimistic over his country's manufacturing future.

Agricultural commodities and manufactured surpluses required markets, and there were many close to home. The British West Indies needed American products, but were excluded from that market by British mercantilist policies. The French colonies in the New World, having re-established trade relations with the United States, were benefiting from this trade. In fact, it helped account for the rapid economic development of the French colonies as compared to the British colonies. The British colonial monopoly's exclusion of U.S. supplies from colonial trade forced Britain's colonies to pay higher prices for all goods. French planters, for example, paid from twelve to sixteen dollars for red oak hogshead staves; British planters had to pay from twenty-four to thirty-one dollars. Indian meal cost the French between $2.50 and $3.67 per bushel; British settlers had to pay from $4.50 to $5.24.[16]

No group of people, however loyal, would continue to pay such high prices without protest, and informed Americans were increasingly aware of the growing need of British colonists in the West Indies for direct purchase of U.S. products. The expensive mercantilist system, which required shipping products to England for reshipment to the West Indies, was crumbling under the pressure of low-cost, direct-shipment goods. Each year various articles of American manufacture were appearing, often surreptitiously, in greater quantities in West Indian markets. Linseed oil, painters' colors, coaches and other vehicles, medicines and drugs, nails and spikes were only some of the products that were beginning to be furnished in large quantities by American exporters.[17]

This growth of exports, so dramatically described by Coxe, was not new. Rather, it was a natural continuation of economic trends from colonial days. A look at the increase in exports between 1770 and 1790 is a starting point for understanding the magnitude of these developments. Exports of bread and flour, for instance, increased over fifty percent. Four times more Indian corn was being exported in 1790 than in 1770, and thirty-three percent more wheat at a time when wheat and flour were key indicators of the economy. The reasons for this are not hard to discover: continuing shortages of grain production in Europe, particularly in France, with a consequent price rise made trade in grains exceptionally attractive and worth the entrepreneurial risks. The rise in prices abroad caused rising prices on the American market.[18] New commodities like peas, beans, buckwheat, and rye entered the market, and tobacco exports showed a yearly increase of almost thirty-six percent; beef and pork swelled the incomes of the American producer. While these commodities increased two and a half times their 1779 export quantities, butter exports increased four times, and rice and potatoes showed a similar increase. Americans now exported as much malt liquor as they consumed—one certain measure of self-sufficiency.[19]

In 1790, Great Britain purchased the greatest quantity of American goods; France and her colonies ranked second despite the absence of a commercial treaty with Great Britain. As Coxe had made clear, the American economy of 1790 was not that of 1770. The youthful nation, now organized under a federal government, was growing swiftly, perhaps more swiftly than anyone on either side of the Atlantic realized. Coxe's analysis had also made it abundantly clear that despite the rebellion and independence, the American economy remained inextricably tied to that of the mother country. In the crises soon to erupt in Europe, in the wars that would engulf many nations and threaten to pull neutrals under, American sympathies might nostalgically fall with France, but economic reality would hold her to Great Britain. Almost half of all exports in 1790 were to Great Britain and its colonies, whereas exports to France were less than half that amount, the balance going to Spain, the Netherlands, Portugal, Germany, Denmark, Africa, the East Indies, Sweden, the Mediterranean, Flanders, and Northwestern America in rapidly decreasing dollar amounts.[20] With the exception of tobacco, lumber, lumber products, livestock, indigo, flaxseed, and potashes, the major U.S. exports in 1790 were foodstuffs. Provisions for consumption fluctuated with European demand, the size of armies, changes in governmental economic policies, and soil and weather conditions. The kinds of commodities exported in 1790 in the order of their importance were: flour, tobacco, rice, wheat, corn, dried fish, potashes, indigo, staves and heading, horses, meal, beef, lumber and timber, boards, flaxseed, and bread.[21]

American exports not only reached new heights in 1790, they continued to soar during the next few years. This quite understandably invited speculation in foreign trade by men fully aware of the situation with respect to commercial treaties, of developing animosities between France and Great Britain, and of the high profits to be made in trade with the Old World. Commerce, or the carrying trade as it was often called, now became the mainspring for agriculture and industrial development and if economic policies and restrictions occasionally seemed to hamper the proper tempo of the works, the demands created by shortages from various causes set it right again. The carrying trade depended upon foreign-owned bottoms, and British interests owned the largest share of them. It would be a number of years before the Republic could boast of its own merchant marine or navy. Some observers thought that America had entered a new economic era and begun to achieve independence from the colonial economic institutions of England. If the "strife of Europe" did not pull the young country into its vortex, they predicted that the U.S. economy, stimulated by supplying provisions to the European disputants, would exceed all estimates of growth.

In addition to the prosperity of the period, there was relative tranquility in politics. In a letter to his friend William

Carmichael, in Spain, Jefferson remarked on the few changes in the recent election and suggested that they signaled the country's entry upon a period of economic and political stability that "augured well for the future."[22] This prosperity derived from the strengthened Government and from the great confidence now placed in it by the citizens. To another of his numerous correspondents, Jefferson boasted that no nation enjoyed greater prosperity or had greater prospects.[23]

Despite the optimism shared by Jefferson and many of his compatriots, Americans were soon to learn that their affairs could not escape being entangled with developments in Europe. By 1791 the accuracy of Coxe's analyses had become clear to many. The American economy was indeed inescapably involved. It was at this time that Spain, France, and Great Britain enacted a series of measures restricting foreign commerce in their colonial and home ports. France limited whale oil and tobacco and levied additional duties on ships. Spain restricted the importation of corn; and England, corn and the size of ships engaged in trade. Such actions threw gloom over the bright prospects of American trade and caused Jefferson to reflect upon the vagaries of foreign governments. Jefferson was, in fact, echoing Tench Coxe's statements and voicing sentiments later to become familiar as Washington's policy of isolation. While holding firmly to his agrarianism, Jefferson developed a belief in the support of industry. He espoused a policy of complete economic independence, which meant, among other things, the development of infant industries.[24]

Many Americans were disturbed by the attempts of foreign governments to control and regulate American commerce and thus interfere with the growth and prosperity of the United States. It was quite clear to these individuals that a system of reliable commercial treaties with other governments was imperative; the accomplishment of this system became one of the foremost aims of the Washington Administration. Particularly struck by Great Britain's policies forbidding American trade to the British West Indies—a business of long-standing and

custom—Jefferson thought that the United States had been
singled out in a most discriminatory manner to be barred from
dealing with its "neighbors."[25] While such commercial restrictions dampened the hopes of some, public confidence in the
future ran high. Funds for the public credit rose almost to par
by mid-July, 1791, and the eight million dollar stock for the
bank was subscribed to upon issue. Wheat crops were abundant and their quality good.[26] In fact, funds for public credit
soon rose above par causing Jefferson to worry about gambling
in public stocks. He feared such speculation would lead to
economic disaster.[27] It seemed that only events of overriding
magnitude could puncture public optimism, but such events
were forthcoming. At first, the French Revolution appeared to
promise an endless market for American products while justi-
fying the American Revolution and reaffirming the rights of
man. But the threat of the French Revolution to order and
monarchy—even to property—called for stern measures, family
alliances, and vigorous action against France by her neighbors.
By the autumn of 1791, for example, Great Britain had
initiated a series of limitations designed to strengthen her
internal economy for the growing crisis. The British shut all
ports to foreign wheat, tightened inspection of all foreign
vessels and their manifests, and impounded ships and cargoes
when irregularities appeared in the bills of lading.[28]

The arrival in 1791 of George Hammond, Minister Plenipotentiary from Great Britain, signaled the opening of long
negotiations between the United States and Great Britain that
were to culminate finally in the Jay Treaty and a new system
of commercial relations between the two countries. Since the
treaties of alliance and commerce of 1778 between France and
the United States were in force, the major commercial negotiations lay between Britain and America. Recognizing the
importance of such negotiations and realizing the need for constant and continuing representation in the courts of the major
European powers, Washington sent to the Senate for confirma-

tion his nominations for posts in Great Britain, France, and The Hague. The President nominated William Short, Jefferson's friend, for The Hague, Gouvernour Morris for France, and Thomas Pinckney for the Court of St. James. His recommendations opened the Senate's first major foreign policy debate. Some senators opposed any foreign representation; others disliked the persons nominated. Morris, in particular, was under heavy fire. After a considerable debate, the senators decided to ask Secretary of State Jefferson for more information proving the need for permanent establishments in foreign courts, and they appointed a committee of five to study the problem.[29]

The committee called Jefferson before it on January 4, 1792. Assuring them that he would give them all the information that he could properly communicate, the Secretary briefed the senators on the world situation and patiently explained why Washington had decided to establish representatives abroad. Since Gouvernour Morris was already resident in France he should be confirmed as minister plenipotentiary (perhaps as an economy move) while no lower rank would properly satisfy the Court of St. James. Spain and Lisbon required only chargés d'affaires, while The Hague would be satisfied with a minister resident.

In this first formal briefing of a Senate committee on foreign affairs, Jefferson cited several new developments that he felt supported the need for permanent establishments in foreign countries. Paris proposed a new and more liberal treaty promising freer commerce; the French Government also planned to send a minister to reside in the United States. London had already sent Minister Hammond, presumably empowered to adjudicate differences that had developed between the two countries since the signing of the Treaty of Paris. Talks about Northwestern posts, Negroes, and other matters were "in train." Discussions about a commercial treaty had begun. Jefferson had indications from Spain that the King was willing to reopen negotiations for navigation on the Mississippi, and Jefferson proposed that for this purpose one of the experienced men already in Europe join Mr. Carmichael in Spain. Furthermore, the Secretary explained Portuguese attitudes toward the United States in the difficulties with the "Algerines," the negotiations of loans in Holland, and the transfer of the French debt to The Hague.[30] In the end Jefferson's appearance before the committee resulted in the confirmation of the nominees. The momentary flirtation with an isolationist policy by some senators in this first major foreign policy debate evaporated quickly.

Jefferson's testimony saved the day for the Administration, although he himself was not happy about the nominations. He had wanted Gouvernour Morris for Great Britain and William Short for France, believing that Short, who had been his secretary in France during the early days of the French Revolution, possessed unique qualifications for the post. When Washington nominated Pinckney for London, Jefferson was nonplussed, though obedient to his President's desires. Thus, a virtually unknown and inexperienced man was confirmed as Minister Plenipotentiary to the Court of St. James, a man whose mettle was soon to be tested in a grave diplomatic crisis.

The abruptness of the appointment left Pinckney only two months in which to arrange his private affairs since it was Washington's desire that he assume his duties at the earliest possible time. Pinckney suggested in a letter to Jefferson that he and his family stop in Philadelphia for a series of verbal briefings before departing for London.[31] He was embarrassed in December by a premature release in a Charlestown newspaper about his appointment, but was reassured by Jefferson in mid-January, 1792, that his appointment was confirmed. Aware that confirmation was delayed, Jefferson explained that the hearings had been slowed down by the debates over the "expedience of foreign missions" as well as by a disagreement over Gouvernour Morris.[32] The opposition to the latter, had, in fact, jeopardized the establishment of all missions when a coalition of isolationists joined with personal opponents of Morris to threaten the "whole system."[33] Jefferson assured Pinckney that his nomination had met with no opposition. In mollifying tones, he suggested that since travel to England was so precarious in January and February that Pinckney might prefer to delay his trips to Philadelphia and to London even to the "Vernal equinox." In the meantime Jefferson would spend his time negotiating with George Hammond, the new Minister from Great Britain, hoping to learn in the course of these discussions in what ways Pinckney could most effectively represent American interests at the English Court.[34]

Actually there seemed no particular need for haste early in 1792 for either Jefferson or Pinckney. The prosperity of 1790–1791 continued and gave promise of permanence. Newspapers hailed the outlook. "Providence, Nature, and Time" had combined to accelerate progress in America toward that millenium dreamed of but yet unknown to man.[35] Following a momentary crisis in 1791, even foreign affairs appeared to remain quiet. In Great Britain, Parliament was on vacation, the naval armaments of 1791 had been reduced and British seamen had been discharged to other employment or to "vice and idleness."[36] The American economy appeared to be bursting at the seams. Specie was more plentiful than ever before. Capital sought new opportunities for investment and for employment. The increase in rents and landed property offered one avenue for investment. In some areas this rise had been precipitate, equaling almost forty percent in a six-month period. The surplus of capital following the early speculations in public funds was turning now to investment in landed property.[37]

In the recurring crises of the next four years, foreign trade was to furnish another tempting outlet for the surplus capital of "monied men." Certainly the import of consumer goods reached new levels in America with consequent effects upon the Old World: Glasgow, for instance, bathed in the reflected prosperity of the New World. For eighteen months, exports of "muslins, and other Scots and English Manufacturers . . . to

America" had improved wages in various Scottish industries.[38] Thus, American prosperity lent an air of serenity to domestic affairs in 1792, and American hopes colored foreign affairs in most promising hues.[39]

As long as affairs remained prosperous and no restraints were placed upon the burgeoning economy, few complaints would be leveled at the Government, and satisfaction would continue high. Minor irritants, to be sure, were under the surface ready to erupt into ugly partisan hatreds and cries of "War with France" and "War with Britain." But on the whole, the early months of 1792 were spent in watchful waiting in Europe, in increased agricultural and shipping preparations in America and, by Pinckney before his sailing date, in careful study and detailed briefings of his responsibilities as the first Minister Plenipotentiary under the Constitution to the Court of St. James.

Beginnings of the
London Mission

II

You know how much the scenes passing under your eyes are the
objects of universal attention. A few lines of accurate information
from you would fill in my mind a space now occupied by contradic-
tory assertions and bold conjectures.

—Pinckney to Morris, 10 August 1792

IFFICULT AS IT IS for Americans today to realize, neither
the British public nor English officials in the 1790's paid
much attention to the domestic affairs of their cousins across
the ocean. A careful combing of *The Times* prior to 1792
illustrates this fact. The little notice given was basically economic: a brief note in early 1792 on the establishment of a mint
in America and from time to time speculations on ways to
improve economic relations between the two countries.[1] It was
almost as though the British did not want to remind themselves of their recent failures in colonial affairs. Rumors of a
new commercial treaty, however, were growing, and Hammond's appointment as Minister Plenipotentiary to the United

States caused renewed interest in the new nation. News about America appeared with greater regularity in *The Times* from 1792 onward—the most significant early item being a report from a committee of the Lords of the Privy Council on the trade between Great Britain and the United States.[2]

Emphasizing the need for new commercial arrangements, the Lords described the economic anarchy which had existed between the two countries while America was governed by the Articles of Confederation. Because of that chaos, according to the committee, Britain had avoided the development of a firm commercial agreement. Since the adoption of the Constitution, however, the situation had changed. Negotiations were now possible and desirable.[3] The committee pointed out a fact generally unknown to the public: British citizens actually owned a substantial share of American shipping. In fact, only New England could boast of an independently owned merchant marine. For this reason alone, a settlement for better commercial arrangements would benefit British citizens.[4] This fact of British ownership of ships carrying the major portion of American goods to foreign markets needs to be emphasized. The import-export data of 1790 showed that British tonnage was far larger in the American trade than had previously been believed, and the demand for grain in Europe since the outbreak of the French Revolution had sharply increased, causing more ships loaded with American corn to move to Europe than ever before. The price of wheat in Europe had doubled the price for wheat in the United States and increased the cost of freight, causing more vessels to sail from Britain on purely speculative voyages. And finally, because of the French Revolution, French colonies in the New World had opened their ports to free trade with the United States.[5]

The changes wrought by the adoption of the Constitution meant a new era of possibilities. The language of the document appeared to nullify the various state laws designed to prevent the collection of debts owed to British creditors and, although the Federal courts had not yet clarified this major issue, the Lords expected the removal of this stumbling block to amicable United States–British relations.[6] While it was true that many conflicts of interest remained, the committee recommended a cautious, experimental, but positive exploration of methods of accommodation. Fully recognizing the continued existence of resentments caused by the American Revolution, the Lords, nevertheless, urged that negotiation be attempted. Time would eventually heal old wounds, and the incontrovertible fact of common heritage would restore friendship between the two countries. Nor were the members of the committee unaware of the pro-British political group in the American Congress. Since the Americans seemed friendlier to the British than many had expected, it would be disastrous, the Lords thought, to provoke animosity by hostile acts. Yet, they urged caution until the effect of recent congressional actions and attitudes could be ascertained.[7] Most important, the committee report, made fully public in *The Times,* recommended reopening trade negotiations provided that traffic to the British West Indies was not ceded to American bottoms. Manufactured articles from America were few and could be easily obtained from other countries. The Lords foresaw no difficulty in controlling the trade of American grain to European markets. From their vantage point American trade prospects looked bleak except for the French islands and Spanish dominions. The Lords expected, however, that trade even there would be curbed by the respective mother country and that the American advantage would prove precarious.[8]

In short, the Lords were willing to reopen the question of trade relations with the United States after careful investigation and negotiation. These were simply policy recommendations, but revealed a change in the British attitude; however, they were not to be implemented for the immediate present. In fact, during the next three years, Britain would be more restrictive than ever before on American shipping, maintaining a closer surveillance of crews whether she had the "right" to do so or not. During the early months of 1792 she kept her ports closed against the importation of wheat and flour.[9] Under ideal conditions it is probably true that some agreement between Great Britain and the United States on commercial relations would have been accomplished within a short time after the exchange of ministers. But conditions were not ideal. The French Revolution and the many events it set in motion were to prevent an easy and quick settlement. Early in 1792 the European powers began to ally to defeat the French Revolution by force.[10] While Edmund Burke's *Reflections on the Revolution in France*, published in 1790, was stirring British public opinion to unaccustomed emotional heights, there was, momentarily at least, some toleration of diverse political systems in England, a situation that would change with events. Pointing to the different forms of government coexisting in the world, *The Times* observed that no one should determine by force which system was the right one. At the same time it feared the explosive nature of the French Revolution.[11]

When France declared war on Hungary in April, 1792, stocks in England fell. James Maury, the U.S. Consul in Liverpool, fearing the impressment of American seamen, warned Jefferson that American shipmasters should take extra precautions to authenticate proofs of citizenship for their crew members.[12] And, although a bill regulating trade with the United States was read in Parliament a second time, that body took no further actions detrimental to American trade except to invoke a century-old act against American produce in foreign bottoms entering Guernsey and Jersey.[13] While coffee house patrons on both sides of the Atlantic in the spring of 1792 drank toasts to better commercial relations between Great Britain and the United States, Parliament extended all existing trade acts for another year. Trade policies with the United States, however, remained to be negotiated during a series of severe military and political crises between the two countries.[14]

Pinckney had settled his affairs in Charleston by April, and leaving his plantation in charge of William Fraser, the over-

seer, sailed with his family on board the *Delaware* for Philadelphia, the point of embarkation.[15] He found himself burdened with a series of miscellaneous chores for friends in South
Carolina, including a commission to purchase a "Grand Piano
Forte" for the St. Cecilia Society of Charleston, and he carried
with him twenty-five pounds for the purchase of "modern musi-
cal productions for a concert."[16] He also took a number of
letters of introduction as well as many personal letters from
South Carolinians to their English families and friends. As a
member of the board of directors of the Santee Canal Company
of Charleston, he was to select an engineer in England to
supervise the construction of the canal between the Santee and
Cooper Rivers, and he was to hire laborers to work on that
project.[17]

Among several who had sought the position as Pinckney's
personal secretary was John Churchman, who, in pleading both
ability and need, sent Pinckney a copy of his *Magnetic Atlas.*
Churchman hoped to make magnetic observations on the coast
of England and to establish close contact with European scientific societies. Knowing Pinckney to be a patron of the sciences
as well as of the arts, he wanted the position of secretary as a
partial subsidy for his scientific experiments. But Pinckney had
already settled on a secretary, a fellow townsman, William
Allen Deas.[18]

Such obligations and problems as these were routine for
anyone in Pinckney's position. When he arrived in Philadelphia the real preparation for his London mission began. In
addition to holding conversations with Jefferson, Pinckney received written instructions from him and was handed a letter
of credence to the King of England and a sealed letter for the
Queen. Pinckney's instructions were sketched in general terms.
He was cautioned to show a sincere friendship for the English
nation and for its Foreign Minister, Lord Grenville. His tone
and his actions should, at all times, be conciliatory. He was not
to meddle in the internal policies of Great Britain by word or
act, but reflect the policy of the U.S. Government which would

maintain hands off in such matters. Commerce was to receive his greatest attention. He was told to champion the cause of American trade to the British West Indies at every opportunity.[19] As for his duties, Pinckney was to coordinate all consular reports in Great Britain and in Ireland. He was to handle all funds for these consular officials and to judge the efficacy of all of their financial claims against the United States.[20] (Pinckney's own salary was to be nine thousand dollars per year, a generous amount for the times, but later to prove insufficient.) The journals of the "ancient congress," the laws and journals of the present sessions, the "gazettes and other interesting papers" and periodic letters relative to his mission from the Secretary of State would be sent to Pinckney who, in turn, was to report once a month to Jefferson on interesting occurrences in England and general affairs in Europe and forward to the State Department periodicals from which the Secretary and the Administration could determine the direction of British affairs.[21] Pinckney was also given the letters of appointment for John Paul Jones as negotiator with the Algerines and as United States Consul in Algiers.[22] Among his other miscellaneous chores was that of procuring workmen and artists for the United States Mint even if it meant asking Gouverneur Morris to search for them in France.[23]

Thus, in conversation and by written instruction, Pinckney's responsibilities were defined. While serving as an intelligent observer of events in Great Britain, he was to remain impartial, avoiding involvement in the internal affairs of that country. He was specifically charged with protecting American commerce and seamen, and in these matters he could threaten retaliation should it become necessary. Here Jefferson must have had in mind the successes of American privateers during the American Revolution, for the United States certainly had no navy. He was to promote, if he could, trade for American ships with the British West Indies. He was to coordinate and centralize under his direction the activities of all the U.S. Consuls in Great Britain and Ireland, and to strengthen this power he was given financial authority over these consulates. Now fully prepared, Pinckney was ready to enter upon his assignment as Minister Plenipotentiary to Great Britain.

Whatever costs accrued to Pinckney in his exertions on behalf of impressed American seamen were to be charged to the Executive Department. It was the area of impressment which Jefferson feared might cause the greatest difficulty between the two countries, and he urged Pinckney to lose no time in developing some permanent agreement which would protect U.S. citizens from this danger. He did not regard as workable Gouvernour Morris' idea of requiring Americans to carry certificates of citizenship with them, for this would give the British Government legal authority to seize all seamen without such papers, and seamen were notoriously absent-minded about such matters. Jefferson preferred the development of a formula based upon limitation of the number of seamen according to the tonnage of the vessel. No press gangs would be allowed aboard unless the size of a crew was above a certain ratio, in other words, unless there was reason to suspect the presence of impressment dodgers. Jefferson insisted, too, that an American consul, at least, should be present at such searches in port. Furthermore, Pinckney was instructed to describe to Lord Grenville the irritation caused in the United States by the impressment of American seamen and to remind him that even the mighty British fleet could hardly prevent reprisals if such practices were not stopped. It was Jefferson's hope that the two Governments could reach a speedy agreement on this particularly troublesome matter.

On June 25, 1792, "a time for better sailing" that Jefferson had recommended, the Pinckney family embarked for London from Philadelphia on board the *Ceres*. Provisions for the voyage included a milk cow (so that the six Pinckney children would have an adequate diet), limes, pineapples, yams, potatoes, meat, livestock, and flour. There would be freshly baked bread each morning. Whereas by modern standards the cuisine might lack magnificence, it was nutritious, though troublesome and costly. (The size of his family was an important reason for Pinckney's expenses exceeding his expectations.)[24]

The voyage lasted thirty-eight days. Arriving in London early in August, Pinckney found letters from America informing him that the President and the Secretary of State had left Philadelphia for the summer. He could not expect any dispatches from his Government until early October. At the outset of his mission, therefore, Pinckney was left to his own devices. He was assured that nothing of great moment had happened in America since his departure, except that a new protest had been received from Hammond regarding the Vermont boundary lines.[25] A letter from his brother, Charles, told Pinckney of Deas' acceptance of the position as secretary to the mission. Deas was to await Pinckney's signal to sail, thus delaying him and forcing Pinckney to function for the first few months of his mission without secretarial help.[26]

Pinckney settled his family in a commodious house on Hertford Street in Mayfair and paid his official calls upon members of the British Cabinet. Unfortunately, he had arrived at the season when government officials were on holiday in their country houses. Lord Grenville, newly married to Lord Camelford's daughter, was honeymooning at his country villa, an elaborate establishment that was extravagantly described in the columns of *The Times*. Pinckney found only the Lord Chancellor, the Duke of Portland, Lord Salisbury, and Mr. Windham at home.[27] Much of the remainder of the time he spent with his family in visiting famous London sites, pointing out to his wife and children places where he had lived and studied, introducing the family to friends of earlier days, equipping and furnishing their London house, and arranging for nurses and teachers for the children. In fact, Pinckney sent Gouvernour Morris scurrying about Paris purchasing china, glasses, and wine for the London residence.[28]

Once settled in his legation, Pinckney wasted little time in contacting Morris. In their first correspondence he discovered to his surprise that William Short was still at The Hague. Pinckney thought Short had already gone to Spain to aid Carmichael in his negotiations on the navigation of the Mississippi, but Short's commission for that assignment had not yet arrived.[29]

The new Minister Plenipotentiary must have felt lonely. He was without a secretary, he could expect no instructions or guidance until October and there were no British officials available with whom he could open negotiations. He could spend his time, however, following developments in Great Britain and familiarizing himself with the situation in Europe. The news in England was encouraging to his mission, and funds had risen in response to the British successes in India, money was abundant, and hopes were high that the mid-year economic tremor foreshadowed nothing worse.[30]

The established order of monarchy and property continued to receive the enthusiastic support of *The Times*.[31] That august newspaper even noticed, although briefly, the arrival of a new Minister Plenipotentiary from the United States. Withal it could not help expressing, however subtly, the natural distrust of the young Republic felt by a nation devoted to monarchy and aristocracy.[32]

As British officials began to return from their holidays, Pinckney was met by J. B. Burgess, Undersecretary of State for the Foreign Department and an English schoolmate of Pinckney's before the American Revolution.[33] At Whitehall Burgess introduced his friend to Lord Grenville, who told Pinckney that he would be presented to the King at a levee on the following Wednesday.[34] In this first meeting between a British foreign minister and an American ambassador, Pinckney assured Grenville of the friendly feelings of his Government and in turn received similar assurances from the British official. Furthermore, Grenville instructed Pinckney on the protocol to be observed when presenting his credentials to the King and Queen.[35] That Pinckney was a personal acquaintance of Burgess undoubtedly helped to thaw the chilly disposition of the British Foreign Office.

Thus, on August 8, 1792, at a "very thinly attended" levee at St. James, the Pinckney mission officially began. Immediately thereafter, the King, like his Cabinet, fled to the country. Pinckney was left to survey at his leisure the problems arising from American and British relations with France and with each other and to attend to the routine of his London establishment.[36]

Pinckney's introduction to the Court coincided with the beginning of a serious deterioration in the relations between France, Great Britain, and the United States. In solemn tones *The Times* decided that "Mr. Burke's predictions in respect to France are all fulfilled."[37] Pinckney scanned the daily columns of *The Times* and other British publications, but not limiting himself to those sources of intelligence, he initiated a long and continuing correspondence with his counterpart in Paris. The Pinckney–Morris correspondence became a most significant link in America's outer chain of diplomatic representation. The two Ministers were cooperative and in general agreement upon the basic points of American policy and interests; too, Morris shared with Pinckney his impressions of the London political world, gleaned from service in London during the early 1790's, and Pinckney relied heavily upon Morris' interpretations of developments in France.[38]

As Morris related to Pinckney, commercial relations between the United States and France were nonexistent. When Jefferson had served in France he had obtained successes in trade negotiations in everything except for American salted provisions, tobacco, tar, pitch, and turpentine. William Short, Jefferson's temporary successor, had continued to press for free trade in these commodities as well, but without success. As matters stood now, the recently adopted tariff in France wiped out all earlier gains, and Morris was faced with the problem of reopening negotiations on a broad commodity front. Jefferson sent Morris instructions stressing the importance of American trade to French posessions in the New World. Morris was to encourage the French Government to move its negotiations on a trade treaty to Philadelphia.[39] Of the French political situation in the summer of 1792 he could report to Jefferson only that it was gloomy. Affairs in the French nation, he wrote movingly, were ominously quiet, like "cattle before a thunderstorm." Men, in and out of the French Government, were divided against one another for and against the old government as well as the new. Moderate men were too few to prevail against what Morris feared was the impending tragedy.[40] As he prophesied to both Jefferson and Pinckney, Morris felt the tragedy of the situation keenly because he believed that the opportunity to liberate mankind had passed, perhaps forever. There can be no doubt that Jefferson, Pinckney, Morris, and other Americans shared a sympathy for "respectable" revolutions, but the extent to which any of them might approve of chaos was another matter. Initially, Pinckney was favorably disposed toward the French Revolution, but his attitudes gradually changed as a result of Morris' pessimistic reports over the next few months. In mid-August, for example, Morris described the great legislative struggles transpiring in then-divided France. In this case it proved to be a victory of the legislative over the executive. Morris, a philosophical liberal, but a social conservative, despaired at the disorder, and mourned that it was "a painful Reflection that one of the finest Countries in the World should be so cruelly torn to Pieces." Americans, more than any other people in the world, sympathized with France, Morris admitted, but they could not admire despotism of any sort.[41]

As French political affairs degenerated into anarchy, Pinckney's own position in Great Britain became more sensitive. He represented, after all, the nation that was thought by many Britons to have opened Pandora's Box of revolution. There were many, indeed, who feared a coalition between France and the United States, who had, in recent memory, been partners in the American Revolution. *The Times* in particular expressed this fear in many forms during the succeeding days of uncertainty. Such doubts could only be dispelled by the issuance of a firm neutrality statement from the United States Government; meanwhile, British policy would continue to be guided by its own self-interest.[42] American intentions were further suspect when reports were widely circulated in London of a commercial treaty between Spain and the United States giving the latter free navigation rights on the Mississippi.[43]

Aside from routine affairs of the mission (and these were considerable), Pinckney was preoccupied with the rapidly changing events on the Continent and in London. He spent a great deal of time supervising the Consuls under his direction, thus learning about their difficulties in dealing with British officialdom.[44] But no occasion arose to permit him to broach the subjects of discussion originally suggested by Jefferson. He could only watch helplessly as Britain prepared for war with France and wonder what effect such an event might have upon his position as a representative of a young and vigorous Republic to the Court of St. James, the very center of support for established and hallowed monarchical principles.[45]

Early Mission Problems

III

*Mrs. J. Gibbs has been exceedingly kind to me in going a shoping
(sic) and advising me about my furniture, she spent the day with me
on Sunday & yesterday we went about my Court Cloathes, I enclose
a list . . . I believe I shall be presented in the middle of October.
I wish it was over with all my heart.*

—Elizabeth Pinckney to Mrs. Motte, 3 October 1792

PINCKNEY'S FIRST REPORT to Jefferson described the increasingly negative attitude of the British Court and public
opinion towards the "new order of things in France." His
failures to engage the Foreign Ministry in discussions on
mutual problems he attributed to Lord Grenville's honeymoon.
The British Minister's absence prevented him from considering
impressments, and in view of the marine armaments proceeding apace in Europe, these problems, Pinckney felt, might well
prove critical.[1] Although he might have insisted upon a conference, Pinckney felt that Lord Grenville "might not bring
with him that temper of mind in which I hope to meet him at
a future day." Despite his petition to the British Ministry for
procurement of personnel for the United States Mint, no

answer was forthcoming. In the matter of arranging for money with which to carry on his mission, he had successfully concluded final negotiations with the Amsterdam bankers for funds. He told Jefferson of his correspondence with Short and Morris, complaining as he did so that the avenues of communication were not trustworthy, a problem that plagued all American officials serving abroad in those days. Since his activities were increasing as his work settled into its daily routine, Pinckney requested the immediate services of his secretary, William Allen Deas.[2]

In his first official report from London, written only twenty-five days after his arrival, Pinckney could show no great successes, nor had Jefferson expected any in such a short time. He did demonstrate, however, that he was complying fully with his instructions: he was analyzing affairs in Great Britain; he was tending to the simple routine duties of his office; he had established contact with his counterparts in the other critical areas of Europe; and he had exhibited enough diplomatic sense to know when it was appropriate to broach matters of such great moment as impressment.

Pinckney continued to devote long hours to his assignment. From time to time he was able to interview Americans returning from France on conditions there, and he carefully filed the information away. He used traveling Americans as couriers to insure the safe arrival of sensitive correspondence to Morris in Paris. It was to one of these individuals, Colonel Eleazor Oswald of Pennsylvania, that Pinckney may have issued the first official American passport in London, a simple document identifying Colonel Oswald as a citizen of Pennsylvania and a veteran of the American Revolution.[3] While this action may have violated in spirit Jefferson's expressed antipathy toward passports, it was Pinckney's judgment that the turbulent conditions Morris described in France fully justified the issuance of such papers.[4] In this matter, as in many others which arose later, Pinckney demonstrated his independence of judgment, a quality essential for a diplomat.

Early in September the first major problem confronted Pinckney, and his failure to resolve it illustrates the awkwardness of his position and the natural difficulties afflicting diplomatic establishments abroad. In attempting to leave France for neutral territory, the Marquis de Lafayette was seized and held prisoner by the Emperor of Austria. Some of Lafayette's companions, released from their confinement, immediately petitioned William Short at The Hague to obtain the intercession of the United States Government in Lafayette's behalf on the ground that the French patriot was also an American citizen. Recognizing Pinckney's position as coordinator of foreign diplomatic and consular posts, Short passed the problem to him in London. It grieved Short to refuse aid to Lafayette, but Morris and he felt bound to do so in view of their instructions charging them with noninterference in the domestic affairs of other countries, and he doubted whether Pinckney could do anything either and had so informed Lafayette's emissaries. But Lafayette, remembering his friendship with Pinckney from Revolutionary days, had asked Short himself to travel to London and seek Pinckney's intercession for his release.[5]

If Short were grieved, Pinckney was distraught. To have to sacrifice his personal feelings and his friendship for Lafayette to the broader strategy of his mission to England was almost too much for him. He stubbornly refused to accept the fact that apparently nothing could be done. He framed an official note of protest to the Emperor of Austria which he forwarded to Morris and Short for their approval and concurrence. Its style was simple and its tone conciliatory.[6] It was to be a petition bearing the signatures of the three American diplomats and claiming that Lafayette was indeed an American citizen.[7] When he met opposition to this approach from Morris, Pinckney wrote Short that he was convinced that perfect unanimity had to exist between the three of them before any measures could be taken, and since Morris would not approve, all forms of direct application had to be abandoned.[8] Meanwhile, Short

had discussed Lafayette's fate with the Imperial Minister at
The Hague and received assurances that the Emperor was
holding Lafayette only for the King of France, anticipating
a complete restoration of the French Monarchy. Lafayette, together with the other members of the French Assembly captured at the same time, was soon to be moved to Wesel where
he would be under the power of the Cabinet in Berlin.[9] Thus
ended the first phase of the Lafayette Affair. Thereafter, despite
his frustration, Pinckney could do no more than follow the
course of the matter through information gleaned from regular
diplomatic channels. He had failed a friend, but his failure had
been diplomatic, not personal. Short's voice now joined Morris'
to decry the shape French affairs were taking, and he feared
for the personal safety of the French Monarch and his family.[10]

Beset by the growing volume of his correspondence and the
rapidly multiplying problems, Pinckney's requests for secretarial assistance grew more and more insistent in each report
to Jefferson.[11] His attention to the deteriorating affairs in
France consumed much of his time, but his attention was increasingly drained by a number of miscellaneous matters: when
William Knox, the U.S. Consul in Dublin, returned to America
on business, Pinckney was beseiged by Benjamin Workman of
Dublin who wished to be appointed in Knox's place.[12] Pinckney busied himself, too, with improving methods of forwarding
and receiving mail from England to the Continent.[13] He spent
a considerable amount of his time purchasing books, newspapers, and maps for himself and for the Department of State,
as he had been instructed to do by Jefferson.[14] Such keen attention to his post left the Pinckneys little time for pleasure. His
wife, Elizabeth, wrote complainingly to a friend in Charleston
that they had attended only two plays since their arrival.[15]
Pinckney did manage to keep Morris busy, however, helping
him stock the wine cellar of the London Embassy.[16]

Despite residence in one of the world's major capitals, Pinckney was isolated from news of America. His information
about political and domestic developments was sparse. Not

only had he to contend with the slowness of communications, but he had few correspondents who kept him informed on other than superficial matters. Jefferson, of course, set out to perform that function for all his envoys, ministers, and consuls, and the result was a circular letter that did little to describe political developments in America for officials abroad. This was a tragic, though natural weakness, and it came at a time of growing political tension in American life—when political parties were forming. Pinckney was forced to depend for such knowledge upon letters from his brother, Charles, personal letters from Jefferson, Ralph Izard, and William L. Smith. His brother's letters primarily contained news of plantation and family affairs, though not exclusively,[17] for from him Pinckney learned of a Creek and Cherokee war in South Carolina which was fomented by Spanish and British agents from Florida and the Northwest.[18] Izard's correspondence concerned itself with his son's military education, which he left to Pinckney to arrange, but vital intelligences on American politics were buried incidentally in his letters.

In his mid-December dispatch to Jefferson, Pinckney despondently reported little progress toward the accomplishment of his official objectives, and his report reflected increasing impatience. At a reception given by the King in early December, Pinckney had countered the King's reference to the "differing circumstances of the Northern and Southern Parts" of America as "tending to produce disunion" by observing that, on the contrary, the two sections agreed quite well and that he thought that they would continue to do so. This was the only direct confrontation Pinckney had enjoyed with the King. Although he faithfully attended the Monarch's weekly levees, except for this brief interchange, the King ignored him. Despite the rapidly changing conditions of European politics, the King's courtiers and the other Foreign Ministers, except for the Polish Ambassador, avoided political conversations with Pinckney. The U.S. Minister could explain such avoidances only by the fact that, rightly or wrongly, these Ministers were convinced of America's support of the principles of the French Revolution if not actually of direct American complicity in the convulsions plaguing European politics. For this reason Pinckney was held at arm's length. He had paid a formal call upon French Minister Monsieur de Chauvelin upon his arrival, an incident which might have lent weight to Court suspicions, but he had not seen him since Chauvelin had ceased attending the levees in early August.[19]

It was obvious to Pinckney that his success or failure as a diplomat would depend in large measure upon the attitude of the British Government toward the United States. This left him little room for an effective use of personal charm, were he prone to depend upon personality in diplomacy, so he constantly maintained a proper diplomatic poise. He tried to avoid widening suspicions of America by avoiding discussions of European politics and by maintaining a conciliatory, though independent, attitude during the early days of his mission. While the Polish Minister was very friendly, all the Foreign Ministers at St. James had paid him the compliment of "the first visit."[20]

There was little sympathy in Great Britain for France except, of course, among members of the hated Jacobin societies. Attempts to compare the French Revolution to the glorious English struggles of 1688 were made from time to time, but the editors of *The Times* considered such comparisons invalid, reasoning that in that rebellion the English had reverted to "Constitutional Government" and had established the "true" religion. In its present struggles France had become a "land of the most brutal savages" overturning in the process "every law, human and divine."[21] Such reactions were now Pinckney's daily diet; he read or heard little favorable to the Revolution. Earlier sympathies had disappeared. Even his own views were affected by the consensus around him—so much so that he demanded additional instructions from Jefferson as a guide to his formal conduct.[22] Even *The Times* parodied the *Declara-*

tion of the Rights of Man under the pseudonym of Thomas Paine Beelzebub:

A firm belief that all men are equal—and therefore that there should not be any superiority in the world.

An aversion to the very idea of religion, because that naturally leads the mind to believe in a Deity, and belief in a Deity creates an acknowledgement of a Being superior to man.

An uniform endeavor to subvert every Constitution or Government which places one man in Authority over another.

A belief that nothing is criminal which becomes requisite to carry into execution the system of levelling all mankind to one common standard; and that in pursuing this plan, Rebellion is praiseworthy —Murder an act of justice—Theft a piece of fine ingenuity—Sacriledge commendable—Blasphemy a virtue—and Hypocrisy a fine exertion of the mind over candour and common honesty.

To consider *Magna Charta* as a bauble—the Bill of Rights a farce— all Law as oppression—Trade and Commerce unnecessary—Parliament a Tyrant, and the King and Royal Family as a public nuisance.

To Abolish the Army and Navy—annihilate all Courts of Justice— open the Prison doors—dismiss every Person in office from the Prime Minister to the Petty Constable—have no taxes—pay no rent—and parcel out the nation equally among all its inhabitants.

These are the *Rights of Man* that I wish to inculcate in the minds of my brethren, and until they have spirit to put them in to execution, they never can arrive at the present state of *grandeur* and *happiness* which the French enjoy.[23]

In November Morris had informed Pinckney of overtures between Great Britain and Spain which, on the surface, appeared to threaten American interests. According to his information, Spain and England were allying against France, and the culmination of this arrangement would depend upon what price Spain had to pay for the alliance. If Great Britain were to demand all of San Domingo, Morris doubted whether Spain would agree; if, on the other hand, she asked for the Floridas, he felt that the compact might be arranged. At any rate, he warned Pinckney to watch the British Ministers. From his own experiences in London he believed that British policy derived primarily from the exigencies of the moment, not from any long-range series of plans or philosophies.[24]

As Pinckney, obedient to Morris' suggestion, followed as best he could the course of the Anglo-Spanish negotiations, affairs in France appeared to change for the better. The renewed vigor of a strong executive in France and the military successes won by French arms brought about a growing respect for that nation's power. But where would such developments end? His remarks on these favorable changes in France, in one of his numerous letters to Morris, brought the rejoinder and warning that,

In Italy we mean to push our Enemies hard. . . . What are we to expect from your Island? Will Britain violate *all* her Treaties? There are some of them which grow to her Vitals. Besides which Holland is somewhat Hobby Horsial in a certain quarter. I incline to think that John Bull is somewhat late in the Season. If the low Countries unite themselves to France and she can extend herself along the Rhine you may truly say that the Sun of British glory is set forever and to their glory you may add their wealth too[,] which has for the last five or six years been the principal object of Administration.[25]

How long could Great Britain avoid entanglement in the widening European conflict? Evidently many thought not long, for rumors of war flew thick and fast throughout the British Kingdom and the economy fell sharply resulting in a brief financial panic.[26] The French attack on the Lowlands gave substance to the rumors, verified Morris' intelligence and caused Pinckney to warn Morris that it was his considered belief that England would aid its ally.[27]

If Morris could almost proudly write of the successes of French armies, he was rapidly revising his own sympathies toward the Revolution itself which was turning into a radical attack on human institutions. Men with feet of clay were the heroes of the moment, and despite his deep love for the French, he found it more and more difficult to sanction the social and political excesses he saw on every side. What was needed, Morris believed, was a moral regeneration of French society, but this appeared remote.[28]

Warning Jefferson of the approaching war, Pinckney again demanded further instructions. He told Jefferson of the meeting of Parliament and explained that the intentions of the British Court would soon be known. While press warrants had not yet been issued, he "had taken several opportunities of suggesting to Lord Grenville the propriety of forming regulations, which might obviate the inconveniences our trade is liable to from this practice, and on the present appearances I strongly urged the propriety of something being done."[29] In Parliament the desire for war was intense, as it proved, and Pinckney pessimistically reported to Jefferson that he saw little hope of French moderation preventing the conflict.[30]

As 1792 and the first four months of his mission drew to a close, Pinckney was involved in three additional, major matters: the desertion of an American seaman to a British vessel, secret negotiations with the Algerines, and the broad problem of American neutral shipping rights.

The first of these affairs, the seaman's desertion, strained Pinckney's energy by the bulk of correspondence and representations involved. In a letter to Captain Edward Dowse, the injured American captain, Pinckney described U.S. policy. Although aware of the law preventing pay stoppage when seamen took service in the British fleet, Pinckney felt that there must be some legal process by which such payment would be enforced, and if such legal documents were formally served, the captain should then submit to them. Should the captain or his vessel suffer any ill treatment, he should obtain properly sworn testimony of such acts for Pinckney's presentation to the proper authorities.[31] Collecting all the documents involved in the case, Pinckney laid them before Lord Grenville with his protest.[32] He used this opportunity to present to the British foreign officer Jefferson's plan for an agreement covering impressment, stressing the urgent need for a permanent arrangement.[33]

Though already heavily burdened by matters such as these, Pinckney initiated the purchase of ten thousand dollars worth of copper for the United States Mint.[34] Then, too, he learned from Short at The Hague that his orders had arrived sending him to Spain to join Carmichael in negotiations for the opening of the Mississippi River to unrestricted navigation of American commerce.[35]

Pinckney also became deeply involved in the secret negotiations with the "Algerines." He had in his possession secret instructions for Thomas Barclay at Gibraltar which contained the terms upon which the United States would settle with the Algerians for the return of imprisoned American seamen. After a time-consuming search, Pinckney located a trustworthy courier, Lemuel Cravath of Massachusetts. For his services Cravath received one hundred guineas in addition to his expenses. Pinckney justified this extravagance in terms of the importance of the mission.[36]

Another incident involving an American vessel and crew afforded Pinckney the opportunity to continue pressuring Lord Grenville for a permanent system governing impressments. One Captain Smith had four men desert to a British warship off the Cape of Good Hope. Rather than being impressed, in this instance they had apparently been atttracted by higher wages. Through the intercession of the British commander, the American captain had been forced to pay part of the men's back wages and to give them a promissory note for the balance, even though they had broken their contract with the American captain by not completing their voyage. This case, similar to that involving Captain Dowse, gave Pinckney an opportunity to explain to Jefferson some of the complexities of the general problems surrounding impressment. There was first the difficulty of differentiating between American and British subjects on the basis of appearance or language, and this problem was compounded by the fact that in order to improve their working conditions or rate of pay, some American seamen were willing to claim citizenship with either nation for their own convenience or benefit. Without dwelling on these matters, however, Pinckney again urged on Lord Grenville Jefferson's plan designating a certain size crew to each vessel's tonnage.[37] They had not yet reached an agreement on this problem, but Grenville had assured Pinckney that he would give it his most serious consideration.[38]

As more American ships sailed to Europe than ever before, impressments began to increase, causing Jefferson to ask Pinckney to warn the British Government of the necessity of "punishing the past, and preventing the future."[39] The increased number of voyages were a result of high prices for provisions and the shortages of wheat and flour in both England and France; the situation had grown so desperate in Great Britain that *The Times* worried about French agents who were buying English corn for the French market.[40] These exports were, according to the editors,

to feed the idle refuse of the French nation; who have quitted their ploughs and spades, to take up pikes and firelocks, and have changed the peaceful agricultural system of cultivating the bowels of the earth, to the horrid and sanguinary trade of murdering one another. This is a very serious evil, and requires the immediate attention of Government. The most strict orders should be given by those in power, to prevent this destructive traffick from proceeding further. Bread is now far beyond the price which it ought to be.[41]

France would not benefit from American grain supplies, the editors of *The Times* believed, because there would not be enough surplus to furnish more than the requirements of the French West Indian Islands. This failure to supply the French demand, they hoped, would rend the alliance between the two Republics.[42]

But the scarcity of wheat in England was rapidly realized, and James Maury, the U.S. Consul in Liverpool, warned Jefferson and Pinckney that such scarcity would inevitably open British ports to the importation of wheat and flour. Like Pinckney, Maury urged Jefferson to permit the issuance of passports to American sailors who would soon be caught in the complexities of a Europe at war.[43]

The problems of Pinckney's mission during the first four months from August to December, 1792, were varied and many. His performance in carrying out his duties was correct; if he enjoyed no great successes, he suffered no serious defeats. He had acquainted himself with his British counterparts and had thrown himself into his duties with enthusiasm and intelligence.

Sounds of War

IV

There is not a power in Europe but possesses one common interest to stop the progress of the new political French disease. . . .

—The Times, *8 February 1793*

WAR PREPARATIONS in Great Britain continued. Repressive measures were enforced against sympathizers of the French Revolution while Parliament met in early January under a guard of five thousand soldiers. Workmen busied themselves repairing the Tower of London, and several persons accused of high treason were immediately imprisoned there. Many ships were pressed into commission, and it was generally expected that press warrants for crews to man the ships would soon be issued. Protected now by strong government measures against the menace of internal republican subversion, official opinion in London now shaped public attitudes toward France. Supporters of a war with France increased daily. In the parliamentary debates on the Aliens Bill, a measure to protect England from foreign influence, Sir Peter Burrel called the approaching conflict a "war of extermination."[1] In the series of debates on the French question, members of Parliament were supported by *The Times,* which early recommended land

and sea blockade of the enemy. By isolating France within its own borders, it was believed that the fires of revolution now threatening to burn all monarchies would be prevented from spreading.[2] The Government began issuing contracts for military stores and for transports. Reports circulated that Commodore Murray's squadron had sailed for the Scheldt to support Dutch interests there. All opposition collapsed in the growing tension and excitement of full-scale preparation for war.[3] The passage of the Aliens Bill and of the Assignat Bill was hailed as depriving the "buried assasin [sic] [the secret agent] of his daggar [sic] and the value of his bribe."[4]

Reporting to Jefferson on these events, Pinckney dwelt on his judgment that war between Great Britain and France was inevitable. The impending issuance of press warrants would aggravate impressment problems, which remained unresolved, and war would hamper discussions of a permanent commercial treaty between Great Britain and the United States. Fully aware that primary discussions on such a treaty were being held in Philadelphia, Pinckney expressed his willingness to open similar discussions with the British Foreign Office if he were so instructed. He asked to be informed of whatever discussions on a commercial treaty occurred between Hammond and Jefferson, but Jefferson never honored his request.[5] Pinckney warned Jefferson in very strong terms to be careful in his dealings with the new French Minister, Genêt. He had been informed by a friend, the Dutch Minister, that Genêt was "artful and deceiving" and that it was his intention to persuade America to fulfill the treaty stipulations between herself and France, particularly those regarding the furnishing of supplies to the French West Indies as well as America's defense of those islands if attacked by Britain. Pinckney told Jefferson that he had informed the Dutch Minister that America would maintain its neutrality in the "present disputes." He was not opposed to selling provisions to France or her island possessions, but he did not recommend direct military intervention in the coming conflict.[6]

Because of the grain shortages in England and the fear that French agents would buy up the scarce stores of wheat, the British enforced a new policy preventing the transshipment of grain from England—even in British bottoms. This move was hailed enthusiastically by *The Times*. In early January a British-owned vessel carrying corn of *foreign* origin was stopped by British customs officers from sailing on to its European market, probably France. *The Times,* ignoring the vehement protests of the vessel's master, commented with great satisfaction that the Government "has very wisely thought fit to stop some corn vessels laden for France." According to information received by *The Times,* the ship owners had been indemnified—evidently paid by the Government—the market price of the cargo and some compensation for other charges.[7] This incident and many others soon to follow signaled the beginning of a concerted effort by the Pitt Ministry to starve the French Revolution into defeat. In view of actions soon to be taken against American cargoes in British ports, it is most significant that the British placed their first restrictions upon their own ships, seizing the cargoes of corn and, in turn, paying the owners an officially determined price for the goods.

The first incident involving American cargoes occurred about this time. The American brig *Maria,* captained by William Callahan and loaded with 1212 barrels of flour, was bound from Virginia to Falmouth *and* a market, as the usage of the time described goods shipped from America to British factors who redirected the shipment to the final purchaser. The *Maria* was stopped by British customs officials and detained overnight. Consul Maury reported the matter immediately to Pinckney who responded at once by protesting the action. The protest proved unnecessary, however, for the collector at Falmouth apologetically released the *Maria,* explaining as he did so that his instructions did not extend to American ships, only to British ones.[8] Apparently British policy toward American shipping had not then changed.

The situation regarding American-owned grain cargoes

aboard British-owned ships was different. In replying to a query from Joseph Smith of Bristol about such cargoes, Pinckney reported the result of his conference with Lord Grenville on this subject:

Several items of a similar nature induced me to request a conference with Ld. Grenville on the subject of the impediments thrown in the way of American grain being carried to France but before I had the honor of seeing his Lordship I found the French had laid an embargo on all British Vessels in their ports which was followed by similar Orders here so that I could not with propriety request that B(ritish) Vessels should be permitted to sail for French ports where (as the event has proved) they would have been captured—American vessels were however permitted to proceed with their cargoes to France or wherever they pleased—which I believe, continues to be the case.[9]

Pinckney informed Smith that he was always happy to be "instrumental in freeing the commercial intercourse of our countries from impediment."[10]

Pinckney was at last able to report some progress to Jefferson. His personal conferences with Grenville, of which there had been an increasing number, appeared finally to be bearing fruit, for Grenville had accepted Pinckney's written note of protest summarizing a number of incidents and had assured the U.S. Minister that redress for the grievances described therein were "in a train for decision." In his lengthy report to Jefferson, Pinckney explained the situation in Great Britain most forcefully. His estimate of forthcoming events was to be proved most accurate by the events themselves.

The execution of Louis XVI horrified Great Britain and pushed the English to action. Chauvelin, the French Minister, was dismissed as a final break before official declaration of war. Since the now-inevitable conflict would be largely a naval contest, Pinckney wondered whether American vessels should not be furnished "proper passports" in order that commercial treaties with some belligerents would continue to protect American trade. It was tragic, he felt, that the United States had no treaty with Great Britain as it had with France. The absence of such an agreement would prove most awkward in the days ahead since the British, at any cost, clearly intended to prevent all supplies and provisions from reaching France. Pinckney feared and in fact warned Jefferson that American ships would be stopped from trading in French ports. He pledged to remonstrate vigorously such actions, hoping for the best, but fearing the worst.[11] This lone American in London asked Jefferson for general guidance in view of the changed conditions and begged for a delineation of his conduct in case of war.[12]

The death of Lord Grenville's father-in-law, Lord Camelford, late in January postponed a series of meetings between Pinckney and him at which Pinckney had intended to continue pressing for clarification of British policy in the face of the mounting crisis. As yet, he suspected nothing, particularly since the incident of the *Maria*, which was released without question following his protest. This, he felt, evidenced the good intentions of the British Ministry.[13]

At the beginning of February, the Chancellor of the Exchequer recommended the addition of twenty thousand seamen to the twenty-five thousand already voted by Parliament, and the Administration laid before Parliament all the letters and papers relative to British–French relations. Although Fox vigorously opposed Pitt's war with France, preparations for it continued, and it now began to take on aspects of a liberation crusade. The chaos in France, the massacres and the terror there, and the rise of revolutionary societies everywhere forced *The Times* to justify the English cause.[14]

The embargoes laid on shipping by both Britain and France were viewed as immediate forerunners of formal declarations of war, as indeed they were. While as many as fifty British vessels had been trapped in France by the French embargo, *The Times* complained that only six or eight French ships had been caught by British retaliation.[15] Furthermore, approximately six thousand British sailors were in French hands.[16]

Pinckney's isolated situation demanded that he handle all

matters at this time on a purely *ad hoc* basis, particularly since
negotiations for a permanent commercial treaty were being
carried on in the United States, although the atmosphere in
the British Foreign Office was scarcely one in which sensible
negotiations could be carried on. He could and did, when the
need arose, make representations on specific problems and cases
to the Foreign Office, and he could report some success:

We are about to try in the Court of Admiralty the right to recover
the wages of British seamen, who desert from on board American
vessels and enter into his majesty's Ships of war. The Attorney general is to give his opinion whether an American Master of a vessel
can by legal process in this country compel an American Seaman to
comply with his shipping contract. *These are measures adopted by
this government which indicate an inclination to pay some attention
to our rights.*[17]

British customs now began tightening its security, and Pinckney found it necessary, for instance, to complain on behalf of
an American citizen who had been summarily relieved of several packets, one of which had not been returned.[18] The
mounting hysteria in London caused other U.S. citizens to
turn to their Minister for aid. Thomas Lloyd, although already
serving a sentence in Newgate Prison for debt, was accused of
inciting the inmates to rebellion and forced to sit an hour in
the pillory at the Royal Exchange. He requested Pinckney's intercession, a request which Pinckney felt he could not fulfill.[19]
New customs restrictions were causing Maury much difficulty in
Liverpool. A list prohibiting the shipment of strategic goods
had recently been circulated to British customs houses, and the
enforcement of the new regulations delayed sailing for a number of American ships. Maury had filed applications with the
Boards of Admiralty and the Privy Council for permission to
permit the export of these strategic items, and he asked Pinckney to lend his support to the applications.[20]

A problem of greater moment, however, now faced Pinckney
.and the Consuls under his direction. According to the twenty-

fifth article of the Treaty of Commerce with France, in the event of war U.S. vessels were to be furnished with passports which would identify them as American-owned. More than forty American ships at Liverpool were ready to depart in February. Obviously, the threat of open hostilities between Great Britain and France caused great concern among the American captains bound for French zones.[21] They demanded passports for their vessels as stipulated by the Treaty, and Consul Maury urged Pinckney to make signed blanks available for this purpose.[22] At the same time Pinckney began to receive requests for passports from many individuals.[23] As the demand for passports for American vessels was too great for Pinckney to ignore or deny, he began issuing them through U.S. Consuls, requiring that very strict procedures be followed in determining the nationality of the owners of each vessel.

Reporting to Jefferson on his actions in issuing passports, Pinckney described the great demand and explained that the passports he had issued were "conformable to our treaties of commerce." Another justification for their issuance, he argued, was that Lloyds of London granted lower rates to American cargoes and ships when protected by a passport. Finally, while doubting the "strict right" of anyone outside the United States to do so, he had granted passports because he felt that they would do no harm. He worried about the format, for it had been developed in haste, and sent copies to Jefferson and Morris for their suggestions. He hoped that Morris would furnish him with a copy of the passport form suggested by the Franco-American Treaty.[24]

Since Pinckney had proceeded so far in issuing passports to vessels sailing from British ports, Morris thought that the system should be continued, despite his general opposition to passports.[25]

It should be emphasized that Pinckney was not indiscriminate in issuing passports to American vessels. In one instance, when the ship's master failed to obtain the signature of the Secretary of the Treasury on the ship's register, Pinckney refused to issue the passport, and he cautioned Maury and Joshua Johnson to watch for this kind of oversight.[26] Knowing Jefferson and Morris' attitude toward passports, when it appeared necessary to furnish them to American captains, Pinckney took firm and decisive action but kept his superiors and peers informed.

Meanwhile, in an editorial on the approaching war, *The Times* observed a coalition among the monarchies:

There is not a power in Europe but possesses one common interest to stop the progress of the new political French disease; and the People are equally bound to secure themselves from this pestilential contagion, which for four years past has desolated the finest kingdom in the universe.[27]

Contrary to some of the arguments advanced by opponents of the war, *The Times* staff believed that great commercial advantages would ultimately accrue to Great Britain if it destroyed the naval power of France.[28] *The Times* hailed Grenville's firmness in the Foreign Office:

We were neither to be threatened into a neutrality, nor argued out of that which it was just to accomplish. France has nothing now to hope from negotiation.[29]

The formal declaration of war was delivered to Parliament on February 12, 1793. What Pinckney had feared had come about. Great Britain and France, traditional rivals, were at war again.

Insurance rates immediately rose causing consternation among merchants engaged in Anglo-Franco-American trade. As William Vaughan explained to Pinckney, what was needed to lower these exhorbitant rates was a statement from the French Government that it would respect the neutrality of American ships. If Pinckney could obtain a clear statement of intent from the French, Lloyds, among others, would be reassured, and the rates would decline.[30]

The war quickly affected several other branches of the British economy: Many mercantile houses stopped payment and closed their doors, although the larger houses that failed were principally engaged in brokerage and insurance in West India.[31] Panic continued for the next few months, adding to the uncertainty of the period. Efforts to obtain crews for British ships led to furious activities by press gangs in all of the English coastal cities and to tense relations between Britain and the United States, as many Americans found themselves inducted into British naval service. Indeed, British and American sailors sometimes joined in fighting off press gangs.[32]

If impressment were to be a continuing problem for Pinckney in the next few months, the gravest problems were those concerned with ship and cargo seizures by the British. Such problems were to prove exceedingly complex and varied, as in the cargo seizure of the *William,* out of Baltimore. Thomas Young, master, having sailed with a cargo of wheat consigned to Messrs. Pedder & Cotter of Cork, for orders to a final port, encountered storms that damaged his ship causing him to lay over for repairs. His crew, except for the mate, boatswain, and steward, deserted. Undermanned, his ship and cargo were seized by customs officials when they detected grain being stolen from the ship. Young asked Pinckney's help in filing a claim for the ship and cargo before the twenty-one days allowed for filing elapsed.[33]

In France Morris worried about British policies toward American shipping, for he foresaw an effort by Britain to halt all ships bound to France. It was likely that such ships would be seized, taken to England, and their cargoes confiscated by the British Government.[34] Almost simultaneously, customs officers in Liverpool reinterpreted their previous instructions, now applying the nonexportation of the enumerated strategic goods to American bottoms. This was to be a most serious complication, for, according to Maury in a message to Pinckney, all American vessels loaded for sailing in Liverpool had contraband articles on board. Under the new interpretations these were liable to seizure.[35] Thus, it appeared to most American

observers that U.S. shipping was to become a victim of changing events. Whether American neutrality could be preserved
under such conditions by mere diplomatic representation could
be answered only by developments.

Earlier when war had appeared imminent, Pinckney had
dogged Grenville insisting that "equitable regulations concerning Seamen" be adopted. At one of his January sessions Pinckney had been assured that the matter was under consideration
and that such arrangements might be reached at an early date.
Grenville explained to the impatient American diplomat that
impressment was really the concern of another department, but
that he would attempt to arrange for discussions with Pinckney.[36] By this time Pinckney had learned that British bureauc-
racy moved slowly.

As previously indicated, impressment had now become a
problem of the first magnitude. American sailors *"not American born,"* even though long-term residents and veterans of
the American Revolution, were not immune from impressment regardless of any protections issued by U.S. officials.[37]
Only native-born Americans were respected by the press gangs,
and proof of birth, particularly unless carried on their persons,
was to present an insurmountable problem. American ship
captains were warned by the Collector of Customs not to carry
persons without such proof out of the harbor, even though
previous custom-house examination admitted them to be U.S.
citizens.[38] In fact, the most difficult problem facing American
shipping in early 1793 concerned seamen. Some were being
impressed by British press gangs, and others, in rather large
numbers, were deserting to the British navy for the high boun-
ties offered to volunteers.

In February, true to his pledge to arrange discussions on the
subject, Lord Grenville appointed Phineas Bond to open
negotiations with Pinckney for permanent settlement of impressment matters.[39] Pinckney, of course, was delighted and,
after congratulating Bond upon his appointment, arranged for
their first meeting at Cumberland Place on the following Tues-

day at twelve o'clock.[40] The long, inconclusive conference revealed to both Pinckney and Bond the vast underlying complexities of a problem which appeared, on the surface, a simple matter. The entire negotiation turned upon the adoption of articles which would bind each nation reciprocally. The main obstacle appeared to be that while Great Britain made a practice of impressing seamen, America did not. When no compromise appeared to be forthcoming, Pinckney in desperation threatened to impress British sailors as a retaliatory measure unless Britain stopped its own "peculiar" practice.[41] This single meeting between the British and American representatives on impressment was the first and last. Without warning Bond sailed for America where he served as Consul General for the middle and southern states. Formal discussions in Britain regarding reciprocal regulations on merchant seamen were suspended indefinitely. No permanent arrangement would be adopted particularly now that war was a reality, though Pinckney would protest individual cases of wrongful impressment, and often be completely successful. The great difficulty surrounding the impressment problem is more fully realized if it is remembered that this British practice constituted one of the causes of the War of 1812. It was not a matter which would be settled by a few conferences in London in 1793 when England was preparing for war in which emergency action would be dictated by need.

In retrospect, it should be emphasized that the problems arising from British impressment practices were not entirely the fault of the British. For example, six crew members of the *Fanny* were impressed on its outward voyage *with their consent*. Apparently there were Americans willing to swear oaths of citizenship according to the rate of pay offered for their services.[42]

Convinced finally that he could only deal with cases of impressment on an *ad hoc* basis, each case being considered on its own merits, Pinckney's attention was demanded by the problem of the seizure of American ships and American cargoes. Difficulties arose at Bristol. Merchants there, although grateful for the passports issued to their cargo vessels, objected to the fees Consul Davis charged for separate passports. Davis turned to Pinckney for an interpretation of this procedure and inquired whether he might not issue protections against impressment.[43] Pinckney protested a number of British infractions, including a duty imposed upon the importation of tobacco into London. Increasingly concerned about accumulating evidence that the British were not going to respect American neutral rights, Pinckney, in February, carried to Grenville his protests on the larger subject of American commercial rights only to be reassured by the British Minister that American grain in American bottoms would not be stopped.[44]

On March 22, 1793, however, the American ship *Nancy* was stopped below Gravesend, despite having been cleared for sailing at customs and despite the fact that its cargo contained none of the listed prohibited articles. Peter Sharp, master, and Robert Christie, factor, immediately applied to Pinckney for assistance in procuring the *Nancy's* release.[45] Pinckney at once began relaying this information about British policy to American merchants and their British partners. He also informed Messrs. Willink & Company of Amsterdam that American vessels could enter all but "beseiged ports." He based his opinion upon Grenville's promises and his own interpretations of international law.[46] Meanwhile, American vessels halted by the restrictions placed on the enumerated articles had actually been released for sailing from Liverpool. Thus far, at least, British officials were accepting the principle of American neutral rights.

The question of France's attitude toward U.S. neutrality besieged Pinckney in a number of letters from American mercantile houses, and he queried Morris in Paris for his views.[47] He also asked Edward Dowse in Ostend to question French Consul de Bays about his country's intentions, and the Consul explained to Dowse that a decree of February 19, 1793 had thrown open all ports in the French colonies to American ships except that France, like Britain, would permit no contraband traffic to England.[48] Morris informed Pinckney that in his opinion the French *would* respect American neutral rights in the war that had just begun.[49] He went on to warn Pinckney of the intentions of French Minister Genêt, who, according to Morris, carried with him to America three hundred blank commissions for privateers to be given to Americans in an effort to involve U.S. citizens, if not the nation itself, in the war with Great Britain, "a detestable project."[50] Some sailors who claimed to be Americans had already been captured on British vessels, but Morris showed little sympathy for such men. He thought that to execute them as pirates would discourage Americans from becoming involved in the war against the wishes of their Government, but he believed that only a declaration of strict neutrality by President Washington would prevent America's involvement in the war and insure the United States' survival.[51]

In London commercial establishments continued to close their doors in the widening financial panic.[52] While bankruptcy afflicted many, Parliament debated proposed measures to control insurrections and punish seditions, though not completely silencing the increasingly loud demands for parliamentary reform.[53] Expenditures by the Crown for military establishments grew rapidly. Planned naval and army expenditures in 1793 were to exceed those in 1792 by more than two million pounds for each service component, a total of over four million pounds more than parallel expenditures in 1792.[54]

Reportedly, a fleet was setting out to take possession of the French windward islands—a seizure which Pinckney hoped would not force America into the conflict because of the mutual defense clause in the French Treaty. As he reported to Jefferson, Pinckney had continued to press for the observance of American shipping rights for vessels sailing under the United States flag:

I have as yet received no official information of any of the belligerent powers having stopped our vessels bound with grain going to the ports of their enemy; but I anxiously expect your instructions on this subject, which I hope will meet the question in various points of view: till I receive them I mean to contend for the amplest freedom of neutral bottoms.[55]

Slow communications handicapped Jefferson and Pinckney; news of European affairs in America lagged behind the actual events by several weeks. For example, notice of Louis XVI's death by guillotine on January 21, 1793, did not appear in the Philadelphia *Gazette of the United States & Daily Advertiser* until March 20, 1793,[56] a delay which was to cause great difficulty for Americans and British in the months immediately ahead. Lawmakers of both nations were forced to act on old information without knowing for several weeks what effect their actions would have. Pinckney's position would have been difficult under the best of circumstances, but his isolation during the following months forced him to redouble his efforts to protect American interests and caused him to make a number of independent decisions of great import to the relations between Great Britain and the United States.

Meanwhile a bill was introduced into Parliament attempting to stop sending American vessels to England *and* "a market." Such a measure would have serious effects on the British factors because any British citizen ordering American vessels carrying flour and rice to France would be accused of high treason. When Pinckney heard of the bill, he helped organize American and British merchants against it,[57] but their efforts proved fruitless. The American merchants marched in protest to confront Pitt on April 4, 1793, but their attempt proved unavailing. Gloom descended on the former hopes of quick and easy profit envisioned by many Americans and their British partners.[58]

It now appeared to Pinckney that British policies toward the neutrality of American shipping were undergoing a reappraisal, and he began frantically trying to uncover the direction in which they were tending.

British Depredations

V

I find that instructions are preparing to be given to the commanders of His Majesty's vessels for their direction with respect to the vessels of neutral powers and that copies of the directions will be given to the ministers of such powers.

—Pinckney to Joshua Johnson, 4 April 1793

E NGLAND had an uncommonly wet year in 1792. It rained for two hundred and sixty-three days, and the downpours continued into the first months of 1793. As a result, grain was scarce. In Cornwall, for example, although prices for tin were at historic highs and full employment characterized the local economy, the lack of wheat and flour was widely felt, and rebellion threatened.[1] However, the grain shortage in Cornwall and the rest of Britain was soon to be alleviated by new government policies for the procurement of American corn, wheat, and flour touching British ports.[2] The solution was relatively simple: the British would seize the cargoes of all vessels containing grain and, at their leisure, pay for them what they considered a "fair market price." Although these seizure-purchases would temporarily solve the problems of grain supply

56

for the Pitt Ministry, other economic difficulties worried the British Cabinet, difficulties perhaps greater in extent and severity than those involved with the grain shortage. Among other things, specie was scarce. Paper money circulated in great quantities. Business failures in London and Bristol totaled about six million pounds. Several banks stopped payment, and business confidence was in a shambles.[3]

The economic impact of the war with France was severe. It was felt in all lines of endeavor and caused rumors of mass migrations to America in the spring sailings.[4] Notices of bank failures appeared in *The Times* with almost monotonous regularity. The monetary depression which swept into Northumberland and Manchester led the local gentry and nobles to underwrite local banks in an attempt to support the injured economy. The crisis was sufficiently intense that *The Times* reported the arrival of a "Committee of Gentlemen" from Manchester who offered various securities to the Bank of England if it would come to the relief of Manchester manufacturers.[5] At last a parliamentary "Committee of Fifteen" probed the causes of the depression and the Government issued notes on five million pounds sterling to support public credit until general confidence in the stability of the economy returned.[6]

As panicky sellers dumped their holdings on the market, prices of American stocks on the London Exchange fell. While the crisis continued there were more sellers than buyers, even at greatly reduced prices. This interrelationship between the value of stock and currency fluctuations further revealed the intertwining of American and British economies in fields other than trade.[7]

Certainly the situation was dangerous to established authority, and it was so interpreted by the ruling classes in Great Britain. To them the French Revolution threatened to destroy all governmental institutions and the economic panic was only one threat. One writer described the atmosphere of suspicion and distrust saying that the "arbitrary proceedings of the Star Chamber" had been reinstituted, and a man could not speak or "scarcely think, for fear of the *Secret Committee of the Lords.*"[8]

Under normal conditions negotiation with the British Government would have been difficult for any representative from the United States, but the economic, military, and social crises of the spring of 1793 combined to make Pinckney's work even more demanding. However, he did not slacken his efforts, but continued to try to gain some satisfaction from Lord Grenville. He did discover that instructions were being prepared by the Foreign Office to commanders of British naval units for handling neutral vessels in the present emergency.[9] By further investigation Pinckney found that that policy prevented the shipment of grain, naval stores, contraband items, or other provisions to France on neutral vessels and that all cargoes belonging to French merchants would be seized as prizes on all vessels entering blockaded French ports.[10] The first part of this policy, that of preventing the movement of various categories of goods to France, was defined by the Traitorous Correspondence Bill which prohibited, on penalty of death, any resident in the British Dominions from directly or indirectly supplying military stores, gold, silver, forage, or provisions of any kind to the Dominions of France.[11]

A committee of American merchants living in London quickly organized to oppose passage of the Bill. The committee, headed by Mr. Hadfield, sought Pinckney's help in preparing their protests to Lord Hawkesbury.[12] Pinckney gladly lent his assistance and stated that all Americans in England were shocked at this threat to American shipping. But despite their earnestness, the committee's efforts failed, and the Bill was passed to halt all intercourse with France. No vessel "touching here and for a market" could go to France.[13]

The British wasted no time in putting the new law into effect. Admiral MacBride stretched his fleet across the English Channel intercepting all vessels headed for France. Neutral bottoms were included in the captures and many such vessels languished in British ports while arrangements were completed by the British to "purchase" their cargoes.[14]

Pinckney followed British affairs closely and reported in detail to Jefferson. There was the continuing armaments buildup in England and confident talk in diplomatic circles on the division of spoils among members of the Combined Powers with England receiving the French West Indies as its share of the booty. Pinckney understood from Grenville that talks on impressment had been shifted to America with Bond's assignment there, but impressment was no longer the problem it had earlier been. Pinckney was taking up each case, as it occurred, with the proper British authorities, and when evidence in a case was overwhelming, he could report cooperation.[15] The question on seamen had given rise to questions related to British interference with American commercial rights. Pinckney gloomily informed Morris that the British would not "acceed to the doctrine of free ships making free goods." If the cargo was French, then it was liable to seizure. If a vessel contained contraband goods, it too would be taken.[16] Pinckney wondered what French reactions to this British policy would be, whether such a policy, if followed by all enemies of France, would actually starve that Republic into submission or whether such measures would merely be matters of temporary inconvenience.[17]

By this time, and after considerable effort, Morris had temporarily succeeded in stopping French violations of American neutrality.[18] It should be emphasized, however, that this was the period of France's most intense effort to ally with the United States in her struggle against Great Britain and the Combined Powers. Genêt arrived in Charleston, South Carolina, in April, shortly after news of Louis XVI's decapitation was published in America. His reception, though somewhat cooled by the shocking news, was still enthusiastic in some quarters. From the beginning, however, Morris and Pinckney kept Washington and his Cabinet informed of Genêt's clandestine mission to issue commissions to American privateers. All Cabinet members without exception, then, were on their guard against him.

The negotiations in Philadelphia between British Minister George Hammond and Thomas Jefferson on a permanent commercial treaty, like those between Pinckney and Grenville in London, were dragging along inconclusively, despite the fact that the major discussions were supposed to be those in the United States. Jefferson complained to Pinckney that the discussions had never really begun and that things were still in the same stalemate with Hammond pretending to expect instructions from his Government with each newly arrived packet. Hammond told Jefferson that his ministers were in the country, absorbed in negotiations at home, worried and busy because of the war, or merely concerned with other matters.[19] Such excuses were familiar to Pinckney, for he had received from Grenville the same reasons for a series of postponements of interviews during the early months of his mission. Far greater reasons halted the progress of negotiations in America and Great Britain, however. The Grenville Ministry faced the overriding problem of determining whether America might not join France in its revolution against monarchy, and speculations about U.S. intentions extended beyond official circles. *The Times*, however, reasoned,

Why does not America assist France? The answer is plain. America and France hold different notions of Liberty. The Americans are not so *philosophically* mad as to give encouragement to a people who deny the existence of a God.[20]

Genêt's arrival in the United States, the bringing of several captured British vessels into U.S. ports by the French, the lively protests of George Hammond and the known effectiveness of Morris as Minister Plenipotentiary in France, all delayed the negotiations between Great Britain and the United States. In addition, however, it should be recognized that animosities of much longer standing increased the difficulty of agreement. The retention of the western posts by the British, the incitements of Indian tribes in the Northwest by the British Governor of Canada, and the failure of American debtors to pay pre-Revolutionary debts to British creditors stalled negotia-tions.[21] Although American opinion toward Britain was di-vided, resentment of the British was undoubtedly increasing in the United States at this time. Some still believed in observing strict neutrality in the quarrels of Europe; others were suspicious of the English merchant classes.[22] While Americans debated neutrality or involvement in the conflicts of Europe, Washington, after consulting with his Cabinet, settled the matter firmly in late April with the issuance of the famous Neutrality Proclamation. This Proclamation, popularly acclaimed by a majority of American citizens, accorded with the mercantile interests who anticipated large profits from trade with all of the belligerent powers. The only major question remaining, of course, was whether the belligerents would recognize the rights of neutral trading for American-owned ships.[23]

Meanwhile, Pinckney persisted in his efforts to uncover British intentions toward the United States, although he grew increasingly pessimistic, largely because of his poor communication with the State Department. Actually, he knew little about what was transpiring in America. For instance, he heard about Genêt from Morris in Paris, his brother in South Carolina, and from reports printed in *The Times* and other British journals, but in late April he had had no word from Jefferson since January 1, 1793. On the other hand, Lord Grenville was most successful in his diplomatic negotiations, a fact of great concern to Pinckney, who observed that "If the combined Crowns should succeed against France, it is impossible to tell what their detestation of popular governments, added to the intoxication of success may induce them to attempt."[24]

At this juncture an American ship, *The Brothers,* was captured and its cargo of France-bound wheat seized. Crickitt and Townly, retained by Pinckney as proctors for the American cases appearing before the Admiralty Courts, filed a claim for the ship. A month later *The Brothers* was still in custody, its cargo "heating" and total loss threatening.[25] This incident received wide publicity in London and caused the crystallization of attitudes in England toward America, for more was involved than a mere cargo. As *The Times* described the affair,

A vessel from America laden with flour for France has been captured, on board of which, we are informed, were found letters from the American Congress to the secret Committee in France, offering to protect their trade to their ports, and assurances that they shall meet with every support in the power of America to give them.[26]

The editors feared the alliance between the United States and France which Britain experienced during the American Revolution.[27]

The passport system introduced by Pinckney over Morris' objections, though in harmony with the provision of the Franco-American Treaty, no longer protected American ships from seizure, for the Traitorous Correspondence Bill subordinated it. Aware of this situation, yet determined to provide the State Department with a detailed record, Pinckney circularized his Consuls for lists of vessels to which they had given passports.[28] In America, meanwhile, Jefferson announced that all passports issued in the future would be issued only in American ports and to foreign as well as to domestic vessels. Thus instructed, Pinckney ordered all Consuls under his authority to cease issuing passports immediately.

Pinckney's repeated support of American neutral rights received Jefferson's warmest praise.[29] But the British were whittling away at those rights. Forwarding to Jefferson a copy of the instructions given to British commanders of vessels carrying letters of marque, Pinckney warned the U.S. Secretary of State that, according to the usages of war, the property of all persons resident in France and the property of partners of mercantile houses resident in France were liable to seizure and official condemnation and would be considered lawful prizes of war.[30]

Soon after the issuance of these instructions to British commanders, the number of ship seizures began to multiply. The

Sally, J. B. Griffith, master, loaded with 2,109 barrels of flour and bound from Baltimore to Havre de Grace, was captured in mid-May by a privateer off Guernsey. The captors claimed it as a prize at Doctors' Commons despite the clear evidence of its American ownership. British representatives of the American owners immediately filed for the vessel and its cargo, but the question of the disposition of the cargo remained unanswered. Could the owner order it to any market, or would he be prevented by British law from forwarding it to France? The *Columbus,* Captain Ewen of Baltimore, was also captured by Guernsey privateers. Like the *Sally,* it was American-owned. For their defense ship captains and representatives of American shipping firms turned to Pinckney for clarification of such questions.[31] Unfortunately, he could give them no clear answers at that particular moment.

As the captures of American ships and cargoes increased, their owners or consigners sometimes expected Pinckney to assist financially the suits in the Admiralty Courts; however, since he had no funds for such purposes, Pinckney was forced to refuse. Neither were his personal appeals to Lord Grenville on behalf of individual cases with merit of much avail now that American ships were subject to the legal processes involved in Admiralty Court cases.[32]

Meanwhile, *The Times,* after describing Genêt's triumphal progress to Philadelphia and elaborating on the French envoy's clandestine activities in issuing letters of marque, observed for its readers that those citizens of republican countries who were partisans of democratic government were not to be trusted. They would trample all that was sacred to law and order underfoot. In the event that Americans should begin a privateering war against Great Britain and its European allies, *The Times* urged that all American "mercantile vessels without exception" be seized and all American ports blockaded.[33] England's fear of the United States joining forces with France in a privateering war against British shipping continued unabated. Only the publication of Washington's Proclamation of Neutrality in *The Times* on June 4, 1793 began to reverse the trend of British public opinion, although it was about six weeks before word of American neutrality could reach the British public, a prime example of the difficulties of communication during the period. Ship seizures by the British Government had provided corn for the economy in the period of scarcity, and although the policy threatened to cause conflict with the Americans, it received wide support in Britain. To the British the policy was an enlightened one, for while giving Americans a "fair" market price for their wheat, it also prevented those commodities from falling into French hands.[34] *The Times* could only praise the Government's grain policies as "A measure more wise, more useful, and more popular was never undertaken, and executed by this or by any other Government with better success."[35] If Britain could praise these actions, the American temper was different. Added to the insults and misunderstandings of the years since 1785, Americans now became impatient. British infringements on U.S. neutral rights would rearouse many a summer patriot in June of 1793. Revolted by the "horrid plot" of the British court to violate all laws of nations and American neutrality, one opponent of Britain under the *nom de plume* Brutus asked in the Philadelphia *Gazette* that American retaliation, short of war, be immediate and suggested a boycott and embargo of articles of British manufacture.[36] Proposals of this sort were to receive a full hearing at the next congressional session when Madison's proposals for open economic warfare with Great Britain would be debated and defeated. To these issues was added a growing hostility from Jefferson and other members of Washington's Cabinet at the lack of accommodation of British Ministers Hammond and Grenville. Pinckney's information contrasted sharply with Hammond's statements to Jefferson:

Your information that we are not likely to obtain any protection for our seamen in British ports or against British officers on the high seas, is of a serious nature indeed—it contrasts remarkably with the multiplied applications we are receiving from the British minister here for protection to their seamen, vessels & property within our ports and bays, which we are complying with with the most exact justice.[37]

Decisions made by Washington on the basis of a policy of strict neutrality naturally pleased neither Hammond nor Genêt, and whereas the French Minister foolishly attempted to approach the American people over the heads of Washington and his Cabinet, the British Minister quickly lost favor because of the effects of the Traitorous Correspondence Bill on U.S. shipping—once knowledge of these effects became known in Philadelphia. Jefferson complained to Morris that "The bill lately passed in England . . . prohibiting the business of this country from passing through the medium of England is a temporary embarrassment to our commerce."[38]

Enclosing for Pinckney's information copies of several of the memorials and protests from Hammond, Jefferson detailed the principles upon which the U.S. Government was acting in America toward both belligerents. Half-humorously, Jefferson added that when Pinckney gained an audience to review all American developments for Lord Grenville, he should seize the opportunity to intrude *all* other questions at issue between the two countries. At least, according to Jefferson, that was the way Hammond conducted himself. Since Hammond was relentless in his pursuit of British rights, Pinckney should be likewise. Pinckney was empowered by Jefferson to threaten reprisals if he thought it necessary. Jefferson pledged that he would treat Hammond the way Grenville treated Pinckney in London.[39] By mid-June Pinckney had received the encouragement of his superiors to present the united policy of the United States Government with firmness and confidence to Lord Grenville. Once it became known in England that America truly intended to remain neutral in the war between France and Great Britain, tensions began to ease perceptibly. Economic disorder began to subside, and there were far fewer bank and mercantile house failures in England. An uneasy calm settled as preparations were made for Parliament to be prorogued in mid-June.[40]

Owing to his position and many friends in London, Pinckney had sources of information which were often of great value. For instance, in mid-June Pinckney received a series of notes from Thomas Croft promising very important information for the American ambassador. What he had to tell was so secret that he could reveal it only in person and only in Pinckney's private library.[41] Pinckney arranged the meeting and learned that, according to his volunteer informant, the British had issued to their naval commanders secret instructions which would be most detrimental to American shipping. Reacting quickly, Pinckney delivered a formal note to Lord Grenville requesting information about some "additional instructions given by Orders in Council to his Majesties ships of War" on June 8, 1793. Was it true that these commanders had been instructed to seize all French goods, particularly grain and provisions, bound to France and to the French West Indies in American ships for trial and condemnation in British Admiralty Courts.[42] Pinckney's information and his protest must have shocked Lord Grenville because even the Admiralty Office would not receive the secret instructions until June 28, 1793. As it turned out, Pinckney had, in fact, gained knowledge about the order ten days in advance of the Admiralty.[43]

Since the President's Neutrality Proclamation was now common knowledge in England, these additional instructions appeared to be a British rebuff of U.S. actions. It now seemed to Pinckney that there could be no mistaking the direction of British policy. Others in London would agree with this judgment, and one observer with close connections in high places in Britain, warned his American friends that despite neutrality their commerce would not "receive that advantage from the rupture between the belligerent powers which some have held out to you, since our ships and cruisers are determined to starve out the republicans of France."[44] He went on to advise that

American vessels carrying supplies should arm themselves since "nothing but a spirited conduct will preserve your flag from insult."[45] Furthermore, he noted caustically that the British Ministers were not to be trusted because "They would wreck worlds to gratify their views."[46] Having arranged an early appointment with Grenville to discuss these new instructions in person, Pinckney protested the embarrassments vehemently, although he confessed privately to Jefferson that if the price for cargoes was proper, the policy might still benefit American citizens.

Grenville was surprised at the intensity of Pinckney's opposition and explained that he thought the instructions perfectly legal according to international law, citing Vattell as his authority. He argued that the British had not, in fact, out of respect for Americans, gone as far as their authority might have allowed them. True, grain was now considered a contraband item. Since the French Government was the only importer of grain into France, Grenville believed this policy would soon defeat that Government, and he reminded Pinckney that all property seized by the British would be paid for and that American owners would suffer no loss since freight charges would also be paid. Pinckney described his reactions and arguments to Jefferson:

I urged every argument that suggested itself to me in support of the neutral rights, which I contended were injured in this instance, pointed to inconveniences that would attend the execution of the instructions, and urged that the case put by Vattell of a well-grounded hope of reducing the enemy by famine did not exist, provisions being now cheaper in the ports of France than in those of England.[47]

Seizure of American ships and cargoes in the West Indies by British cruisers now began to occupy the attention of Jefferson and Pinckney. The capture of the *Sukey*, which was carried into Jamaica by its captor, infuriated Jefferson, immediately causing him to request Pinckney to protest this seizure strongly. He told Pinckney to obtain from the British Government orders to their colonial subordinates to prosecute such breaches of conduct and to punish the offenders.[48]

In Great Britain, too, lower-echelon British officials were growing more insolent and less concerned about maintaining good relations with the United States. For instance, Consul James Maury was threatened with the service of a legal process from the Admiralty Court to compel him to testify concerning the papers of an American vessel captured carrying several French passengers en route to the United States.[49] Pinckney instructed Maury to refuse to testify regardless of the pressures applied and to claim immunity as a diplomatic agent of the United States. Pinckney simultaneously applied to Grenville for relief for the suffering Frenchman captured on the American ship.[50]

Summer absences of government officials again interfered with diplomatic business. Grenville was spending a great deal of time building his summer villa, Dropmore Hill,[51] and although he passed a relatively leisurely summer caring for his new estate and avoiding the American representative, Pinckney himself was not able to relax because of the rapidly changing international situation. Also personal affairs, namely the death of his mother, Elizabeth Pinckney, burdened him with sadness.[52] The miscellaneous chores attached to his office now consumed great amounts of time. For example, he continued his correspondence with Madame Lafayette and her imprisoned husband;[53] he spent long hours investigating the financial affairs of the House of Donald, in which William Short had lost his savings;[54] he aided Thomas Lloyd in Newgate Prison by furnishing him with reference volumes needed for his defense;[55] he bought copper for the United States Mint from British firms and processed the necessary export applications;[56] he continued to search for workers and to buy machinery for the Santee Canal Company of Charleston;[57] and, finally, he made extensive preparations to attend the traditional American Independence holiday being held by American merchants at the London Tavern on Bishopgate Street on July 4, 1793.[58]

While involved in this heavy daily routine, Pinckney leased a country house, "Hammersmith Mall," on the Thames, an abode "elegantly furnished, accommodated with large Coach House and Stables, with an extensive garden, grounds &c and with the use of a cow."[59] Pinckney's family, at least, managed to escape the hot summer, but he was forced to spend much of his time in town, particularly when William Allen Deas, after only a few weeks at his post as secretary, returned to Charleston on August 10.[60]

Public opinion in both the United States and Great Britain fluctuated greatly during the summer of 1793. Even though it could not affect official attitudes as much as it does today, public opinion was an indicator of the public mind, and the lag between events and the public's response to them was caused by the slowness of communication.

News of strong actions by the Washington Administration against American privateers sailing under French letters of marque and guilty of depredations against British shipping in West Indian waters mollified public opinion in England.[61] This, together with the restitution of British vessels captured by the French in the territorial waters of the United States, caused *The Times* to soften its attitude considerably.[62] Attitudes in America, too, were improving once knowledge that the captains of captured American ships in British ports were being paid freight and cargo owners were being compensated for the value of their property.[63]

To American Ministers Pinckney and Short there was no doubt about the concerted attempts of the maritime powers to starve France into submission. The evidence was too overwhelming to be denied. Short reported to Pinckney in mid-July what Grenville had already told him in his conference, that Spain would be seizing all neutral vessels bound for French ports. With the arrival of the British fleet in the Mediterranean, the depredations against American, Danish, and Swedish vessels commenced.[64]

Whatever rupture these policies may have been causing in

diplomatic circles, Pitt's policy toward the seizure of neutral vessels trading to France was immensely popular in Britain.[65] But what appeared to be a magnanimous policy to the editors of *The Times* seemed only another form of oppression to Americans.[66] As a matter of fact, actual seizures of American ships were infrequent during the summer of 1793, and Pinckney's discussions with Grenville were animated by his concern for principles rather than with specific vessels in distress. Since the capture of *The Brothers* in early May, a case which Pinckney personally laid before Grenville,[67] only the *Jay, Eliza,* and *Active* had been captured by the British, and the brig *Maria* by a French privateer in July. In view of these facts Grenville failed to see what American rights were suffering much actual damage. As Pinckney described his discussions with Grenville,

I continue to receive assurances from him of the desire of this government so to conduct the measures they think themselves justified in pursuing towards the neutral powers as to render them as little detrimental to our commerce as the State of warfare existing in Europe will admit and on complaint of some irregularities committed by British Privateers he requested me to select some instances where the evidence is clear in order for criminal prosecutions to be instituted against the offenders, in which he promised the fullest support of the law officers of the crown.[68]

Pinckney believed that Grenville was sincere in his statements and that public opinion, too, supported a desire for good relations with the United States. He could report that Grenville and his Ministry were prompt in answering his queries, but when it was necessary for him to refer matters to other departments of the British Government, and particularly to the Admiralty, delays were very great.[69]

Having been encouraged by Grenville to put his objections to British policy on paper, Pinckney addressed a memorial to Grenville in which he argued that practice among maritime powers of the last twenty years supported the principle of free bottoms making free goods. He did not agree with the British belief that France would be reduced by a famine resulting from the stoppage of ships to her, for the fact that prices for grain were lower in France than in Great Britain suggested that the scarcities imagined in France did not, in fact, exist. Capturing all French goods on neutral vessels inconvenienced American citizens, particularly those connected with the raising and marketing of grain, and such measures could do nothing but broaden the misunderstandings between the two countries.[70]

Meanwhile, Grenville and his subordinates faced an increasingly grave problem in the West Indies. Losses to French privateers in that part of the world suddenly increased sharply. Consequently, a council was held early in August to develop a means for protecting the British West Indian trade.[71] Mercantilist policies limiting trade in the British West Indies to British ships now began being encroached upon by American vessels. Prices for all kinds of provisions were most attractive, and the need for goods apparently caused British customs officials to permit American shipping access to an area considered by Americans to be one of their natural markets.[72] This development of trade with the British West Indies as a side result of Britain's preoccupation with the war in Europe was to prove helpful in lessening some of the basic tensions which had prevented the settlement of a permanent system of commercial intercourse between America and Great Britain. The situation, however, was to get worse before it improved. Although it was known that the debtor cases in Virginia had been decided in an American court in favor of the British creditors in July[73] and despite the scrupulous observance of neutrality by the Washington Administration, rumors of war between the two countries continued to circulate freely on both sides of the Atlantic. *The Times* denied the rumors vigorously, saying they were being spread by "internal enemies" and that the United States would not come to the military aid of the French West Indies. The British policy of remunerating Americans for their confiscated cargoes should, the editors felt, mollify hurt pride.[74]

Just as it appeared that matters would work themselves out to everybody's best interests, a sudden increase in ship seizures in European waters caused Pinckney to summarize the new situation in London for Jefferson:

I have had several conversations with Lord Grenville but do not find that his government will at all relax in the measures they have adopted toward the neutral nations. I have urged every thing in my power in opposition to the policy as well as the right of these measures, and have assured him that they will be considered by our government as infringements of the neutral rights. As I cannot speak from authority on the subject, I have not said what measures we shall adopt in consequence; although I have strongly insisted on the detriment to the commercial interests of this country which must necessarily ensue from the various impediments opposed to a free intercourse, as well as from the ill will they excite. I may perhaps estimate too highly the blessings of peace in general and the advantages of our neutral situation, notwithstanding all the deductions to be made on account of the conduct of this country.[75]

If there were to be retaliatory measures, Pinckney recommended that they be restricted to commercial matters. Independently, he inquired of the Danish and the Swedish envoys whether they would join the United States in stronger measures, only to discover to his chagrin that neither of them insisted upon the principle of free ships making free goods. They would be content to receive the express treatment outlined in their existing treaties of commerce with Great Britain.[76] If he could not persuade the other neutral powers to combine with America in defending neutral rights, the only course remaining would be to hurry the negotiations for a permanent trade treaty with Great Britain. But the negotiations were delayed, and Pinckney, almost in despair, reported to Jefferson:

I find from official conversations here that the pretence of infractions on our part still prevent the full effect of the treaty of Peace; that a variety of objections to the statement of facts offered by you are brought forward, and that the indecision of the Virginia case is strongly relied upon.[77]

War at Sea

VI

No alteration has taken place since my last in the conduct of this government towards the neutral powers, they still assert the propriety of preventing the provisions specified in their additional instructions from being sent to French ports, and of making prize of their enemy's property in whatever vessels it may be found.

—Pinckney to Jefferson, 25 September 1793

I N AMERICA, French Minister Genêt had become *persona non grata*. Since his arrival in April, 1793, he had caused the Washington Administration nothing but embarrassment and trouble. Naturally suspicious of the two Republics, British Minister Hammond was constantly perturbed by Genêt's actions, which were essentially responsible for the majority of Hammond's flood of remonstrances to the Federal Government. According to Jefferson, Genêt set himself on par with the Chief Executive. He armed vessels, levied men, and issued commissions of war over the objections of the Government, and the *Citoyen Genêt* and the *Sans Culottes* were outfitted in Charleston despite strong protests by Jefferson. Although ordered to leave the port by Washington, the *Sans Culottes* remained in Charleston arming herself, and the *Citoyen Genêt* had the audacity to return to Charleston with British prizes in tow. Furthermore, despite orders to the contrary, the *Vain-quiru de la Bastille* was built in Charleston, the *Anti-George* outfitted in Savannah, the *Carmagnole* in Delaware, a schooner and a sloop in Boston, the *Polly* in New York, and the *Little Sarah* in Philadelphia. All these were instigated by Genêt. Embarrassed, the Government explained to Hammond that those vessels already armed in American ports would be forced to leave them and that no more would be permitted to be armed there. Whatever prizes had already been taken would be restored intact to the British owners.[1]

While Pinckney was daily protesting the British failure to recognize American neutral rights, Jefferson was explaining to Genêt that his objections to British seizure of French goods in American vessels did not actually warrant the United States breaching its neutral stand. It was, in fact, a long-established principle of international law that "the goods of a friend are free in an enemy's vessel, & an enemy's goods lawful prize in the vessel of a friend." The "inconveniences" resulting from halting vessels at sea to search for goods had led many nations in later times to stipulate by treaty that "free bottoms make free goods, enemy bottoms enemy goods." He informed the impatient French ambassador that the United States had introduced this latter principle into its treaties with France, Holland, and Prussia. Thus, French goods found in American bottoms by either Holland or Prussia were considered "free," the very point that the U.S. Government was attempting to establish with Great Britain in its current treaty negotiations.[2]

The response to Genêt on the subject of the British ship seizures was made, however, before Jefferson knew about the orders of June 8, 1793. Upon receiving a copy of the orders, Jefferson angrily demanded that Pinckney exert all his efforts to get explanations from the British Government. Although the Secretary of State doubted their authenticity, he took no chances and concentrated his ire on the first article which stipu-

lated that vessels loaded with corn, flour, or meal bound for
France were to be stopped and sent to any British port "to be
purchased by that Government, or to be released only on the
condition of security given by the master, that he will proceed
to dispose of his cargo in the ports of some country *in amity
with his Majesty*."[3] To Jefferson, this was nothing but a bald
attempt to dictate to Americans what markets were open to
them by the British Government. Aside from the implied insult, Jefferson thought it against the law of nations because it
introduced a practice which, if permitted to stand unchal-
lenged, would damage basic American interests. Agriculture
would be grievously affected, and if agriculture were hurt, all
other American economic activities would likewise suffer. Jefferson challenged the presumption of one nation, no matter
how powerful, to dictate to any other nation to what ports its
produce might go and with which nations it might not trade.[4]
Pinckney was to demand a revocation of the order and to
obtain full indemnification for those affected adversely by it.
In doing so he was to maintain proper diplomatic decorum,
assuring the British of the sincere desire of the United States
to live harmoniously with them. Grenville was provided with
no deadline for the answer, but Pinckney reported the failure
to answer in December, and it was in turn reported to the
United States Congress at its first session in 1794.[5]

In Britain, meanwhile, ship seizures became routine. Owners
and masters of ships already seized, whose cases were waiting
disposition in the Courts of Admiralty, chafed at the restric-
tion. Although Grenville professed surprise at the procrastina-
tion and promised to accelerate the process,[6] Pinckney's hopes
fell. He felt that little room for diplomatic maneuvering remained,[7] even though his representations were not totally without effect as when French passengers captured on the *Aeriel*
were released shortly after Pinckney's petition on their behalf.[8]
    At the very moment of his greatest depression, however,
Pinckney gained a victory of the first magnitude. His persist-

ence in claiming freight and demurrage for captured vessels
was rewarded by an epoch-making verdict in the Court of
Admiralty on September 4, 1793. With pride, Pinckney reported that the Admiralty Court had adjudged freight, demurrage, and expenses to an American vessel whose cargo was condemned under the latest British additional instructions. He
expected that decision to become a valuable precedent, and he
hoped it would decrease the wholesale seizures of American
ships by British privateers. Benjamin Vaughan, a British merchant, congratulated Pinckney upon the verdict remarking as
he did so that he was "more persuaded than ever, that it is
not far distant from the time when negotiations will be
opened."[9] Pinckney did not slacken his efforts after this initial
victory. He collected all instances of seizure of neutral vessels
determined in the Court of Admiralty from previous wars.[10]

Although the decision was undoubtedly a victory for the
American cause, the impressment problem remained unchanged. The British were willing to return all "real" American seamen, but absolute proof of nationality was required.
True, the British did admit as proof affidavits of U.S. consuls
and sworn testimony of the American captain and seaman that
the seaman in question was an American citizen, but there
were irregularities even in this procedure. Permanent arrangements seemed impossible because too many objections arose
to the various schemes proposed.[11]

Capture of the French port of Toulon and consequent British mastery of the Mediterranean posed a serious threat to
neutral commerce. It signaled Britain's mastery of the seas,
and, as *The Times* observed, the addition of half of the French
navy to the British forces could mean the destruction of American trade should that nation ally with France.[12]

In America yellow fever, raging unchecked through Philadelphia, was spreading panic. Public offices closed, and American officials fled to safer ground.[13] A brief note dated September 14, 1793 was Jefferson's last correspondence to Pinckney
until late in November. Thus, because of the time needed for

mail to cross the ocean, Pinckney was to be isolated from official support and advice until early 1794 when Edmund Randolph was to replace Jefferson as Secretary of State. Curiously, however, Pinckney's status was enhanced by the internal crisis in America. When Hammond approached Jefferson about American reactions to the order of June 8, he was informed that Pinckney was empowered to make representations on that subject in London.[14]

Left to his own devices, although unaware that he would remain uninstructed, Pinckney prepared for any eventuality. He maintained a proper diplomatic attitude until unending provocations by the British exhausted his patience. At all times, however, he preserved a proper silence about American intentions. He politely but firmly refused to reveal his intended course of action to all who queried him.[15] Although he doubted whether war between Great Britain and the United States was truly imminent, Pinckney explained to one correspondent that should war come, his Government would want to keep its intentions secret while preparing its defense. He had no information verifying the rumor that France had ceded its West Indian possessions to the United States, nor had he received any protests from Grenville about the French carrying British prizes into American ports.[16]

British privateers continued to oppress American shipping, and although this created uneasiness among the Americans in London, Pinckney continually received assurances that the Americans would be duly reimbursed.[17] It was undoubtedly true that some attempts were made to use American neutrality as a cover for the shipment of grain and flour to France. One incident, in particular, was proof of this. The *Sally*, captured much earlier with a cargo of flour and staves claimed as the American property of Messrs. Cunningham and Nesbitt of Philadelphia, was adjudged in the Admiralty Court. According to *The Times* report, papers reluctantly produced by the captain proved the cargo to belong to the French Government, part of a purchase by the French ambassador on the one hundred thousand piastre credit advanced by the U.S. Government against its revolutionary debt. It was shipped as the property of the American mercantile house "under the expectation of its passing safe under the protection of so respectable a neutral name." Sir James Marriott condemned the cargo saying,

Upon the whole, he had not the slightest doubt, as to the flour being French, but not American property; he did not dispute that the Americans might sell their goods to whom they pleased; but he conceived they were too wise a people to part with their property to the French, in the state of bankruptcy the merchants of that country at present are, without taking good care to secure a previous payment.[18]

From Spain Short reported ship seizures during the summer of 1793 as surely an aftermath of the treaty between Spain and Great Britain. However, the number of ships captured had been small. At the same time Portugal and Algiers had settled their differences through the intercession of the British Minister to Portugal; the effect of this twelve-month truce was to free the ships of Algiers to prey on American shipping in the Mediterranean. The manner of the truce arrangements and other evidence convinced Pinckney that this was a deliberate British plot to damage American shipping.[19] As a protective measure, Pinckney informed his consuls and various mercantile houses of the latest turn of events.[20]

The Algerine truce was nearly the final blow to Pinckney's hopes for negotiation between the United States and Great Britain. His attitude hardened perceptibly, and he approached Lord Grenville with a much firmer mien than previously, although Pinckney had, in fact, never equivocated in his petitions to the British Foreign Minister. During this crisis he received a note from an anonymous woman, the wife of an American merchant, who accused Pinckney of complicity with the British in the latest developments. She pleaded with him to be firmer and to frighten the British Cabinet. At the same time she reported a conversation between her husband and a British Lord:

To the question from my husband, "How they got rid of a late remonstrance from the American States," he replied "Very easy, with fair promises and this image showing him a guinea, he is one of our secret service gentlemen." I suppose he meant you for says he, "Though they dislike Kings, they love his image, besides, says he, we have cut them out some work by sending a present. . . . He said at first the ministry were much alarmed lest the instructions should have been so premptory as to render our key vessels (in danger), However, I could find by their conversation that they were still under fears, lest you should be removed and another sent, for he said some of the Congress had intimated their suspicions of you from your inactivity in their affairs, they had had such a hint from their ambassador! Now as a friend I would wish you to show a little reserve and the next time you may have any business with them show a good deal of resolution, and you will frighten them to compliance.[21]

This well-meaning informant misinterpreted the conversation when she understood "the Lord" to mean that Pinckney was in the hire of the British secret service. Evidently what "the Lord" meant was that the economic motive of gain represented that the Guinea coin served to allay many American dissatisfactions—after all, the British were buying condemned cargoes and in many instances awarding freight, demurrage, and expenses. Furthermore, there is absolutely no evidence or suggestion other than this one note that Pinckney was not completely serving American interests. Undoubtedly, there were also those in America who felt that Pinckney was less active in their behalf than he should have been, but these attitudes were based upon ignorance of Pinckney's activities. The evidence of Pinckney's numerous remonstrances, the careful systems he erected in the consular districts to expedite matters of impressment and seizure, and his untiring efforts to determine as exactly as possible British intentions toward the United States, indicate that he faithfully served the best interests of his country.

Perhaps partially as a result of this anonymous note, Pinckney's determination for a showdown with the British Minister stiffened. He sought explanations from Grenville on the twin subjects of the Portuguese treaty and the retention of the Northwest posts in order "that the real intention of this government towards us might be known."[22] It was a momentous interview. After assuring Lord Grenville of American good wishes for Great Britain, in reply to the sadness Grenville expressed about the yellow fever epidemic in Philadelphia, Pinckney proceeded to discuss the entire range of differences separating the two nations from treaty negotiations. These differences he enumerated as the Indian war in America, a result of the retention of posts contrary to the peace treaty; the release of the Algerines to prey on American commerce and imprison American sailors, a fact accomplished by Mr. Logie, British Consul in Portugal; and the interruption to American commerce and neutral rights caused by British policies.[23]

Lord Grenville, momentarily taken back by Pinckney's hard-hitting accusations, promised a written reply to his protests on the interruption of shipping to France, denied that the Portuguese treaty was intended to "loose the Algerines" (in fact, he offered to permit the Portuguese to convoy American vessels in the Mediterranean), and observed that negotiations on the retention of the posts were proceeding in America. In turn, he chided Pinckney about America's failure to pay British creditors their pre-Revolutionary debts as stipulated by the Treaty of Paris saying that he was continually deluged by "pressing applications from the commercial subjects of His Majesty." As for relinquishing the posts, British frontier settlements would suffer the same inconveniences experienced by American settlements were the posts given up. Furthermore, according to Grenville, Hammond's attempts to open discussions on the posts were greeted in America with blunt refusals to talk about them.

Grenville would have gone on to other points, but Pinckney stopped him, asking quietly that if the United States executed its part of the Treaty by paying British creditors, would the British Government in turn relinquish its posts in the Northwest Territory. Grenville's candid answer reproved Pinckney by saying that "in case one party to a treaty had deferred the accomplishment of their part of the obligation for nine years . . . neither reason nor the law of nations would exact a strict compliance from the other party."[24] Obviously the British Foreign Minister believed that his position was secure, and for the first time he fully revealed British inflexibility. The situation, to Pinckney, had reached the breaking point. He had had enough of insults to American neutral rights. He feared not only that the British would not retract their position on the seizure of American vessels, but that they planned "fresh embarrassments to our trade."[25] As far as Pinckney was concerned, the interview with Grenville convinced him that his usefulness as Minister Plenipotentiary to the Court of St. James was over. If officially withdrawn, he wanted several months in France for the benefit of his children's health, and he requested detailed instructions for the "removal of our Consuls and other citizens with their property and what conduct you observe to the British in America."[26] The refusal to consider ceding the posts was the final blow for Pinckney; now only war could result, and when it came it would be "politic and popular."[27]

Whatever the true intentions of the British might have been as far as the Algerine truce was concerned, the effect on American shipping in the Mediterranean was devastating. In October ten American vessels were captured, and the number continued to increase in November.[28] Contradicting Lord Grenville's statement of British innocence, the Portuguese Minister in London informed Pinckney that his Court had no knowledge of the truce, discovering it only from the Algerine fleet as it was preparing to attack the Portuguese.[29]

Pinckney was not alone in failing to improve the lot of American shipping at this time. In France Morris was having equally poor success in his negotiations, though for different reasons. The chaos in French public affairs made it impossible for him to find anyone with sufficient authority to arrange anything.[30]

To further complicate matters, West Indian affairs now intruded. As instructed earlier, Pinckney had filed a strong protest with Grenville on the capture of the *Sukey*. He had wrung from Grenville the promise that similar violations would be prevented in the future, and Grenville's "fair promise" had seemed plausible because he claimed to be reciprocating for the kind treatment British shipping had received at the hands of the United States Government.[31] In October, however, the West Indies expedition sailed with forty-four ships under the command of Sir John Jarvis and Sir Charles Grey. To celebrate the new adventure, Pitt and other members of the Cabinet were royally entertained by West Indian merchants at London Tavern.[32]

As part of the grand strategy of the British Government, new instructions dated November 6, 1793 were issued to naval commanders. Not made public until December 23, these orders turned out to be the "fresh embarrassments to our trade" feared by Pinckney—further evidence of the accuracy of his intelligence. Moreover, they had been issued shortly after Grenville's promise to prevent excesses against American shipping in the West Indies. The new instructions, timed to aid the Jarvis expedition, stipulated that British naval units should stop all vessels loaded with goods produced in French dominions and that they should intercept all vessels carrying supplies to those places. Such ships would be brought into British West Indian ports for legal adjudication in British Courts of Admiralty.[33] These measures obviously were intended to force a quick victory over the French West Indies, *The Times* gleefully noted.[34]

Thus, in the Mediterranean, the West Indies, and Europe, the actions of the British Foreign Office fell into a clear pattern. American shipping was a primary target. In Britain ship seizures were increasing, and impressments continued to harass the U.S. Consuls. The press for sailors for the West Indies expedition in particular had exacted a heavy toll among American seamen. Pinckney was literally deluged by problems arising from both of these sources of infringement upon American sovereignty.

Pinckney's efforts to obtain explanations of the November 6 orders met only the blank stares of Grenville's subordinates, for it seemed that Grenville was on Christmas leave. Pinckney then turned to his old classmate, Burgess, who appeared to be uninformed about these latest developments.[35] Patiently, Pinckney continued to seek Grenville. His appointment for January 2, 1794 was canceled at the last moment as several previous ones had been. Now even Burgess did not appear to be available. At last, however, Pinckney could take some comfort from the fact that representatives of other neutral nations seemed alarmed.[36]

In the face of increasing protests from committees of American merchants and their British associates, the British Cabinet finally began to yield ground.[37] Pinckney's firmness must also have profited the American cause, for in mid-January he learned in conference with Grenville that new instructions were in preparation. They would rescind the obnoxious orders of November 6 and restore to the United States the privilege of trading with the French West Indies on the same footing as before the orders. Certainly Pinckney could observe a change in Grenville's attitude as he explained his failure to meet Pinckney by the press of affairs relating to the West Indian crisis. The result of the debates was to ease British attitudes toward American shipping.[38]

The new orders Grenville promised were actually issued in Council on January 8, 1794. Instructions were that British men of war and privateers were to bring in for trial ships loaded with French West Indian produce destined for Europe or cargoes belonging to French citizens and ships breaking blockaded island ports or carrying contraband goods. Since corn or provisions were not enumerated as subject to seizure, the new orders represented a major concession on Grenville's part, and he told Pinckney that they were motivated by a sincere desire to retain United States friendship. Never had he been so conciliatory or gracious with the American representative. Pinckney accepted Grenville's assurances with equal grace, maintaining his firm position on neutral rights:

I reminded him, that our ideas differed materially from theirs on this subject, and without repeating the arguments I had before addressed to him both verbally and in writing in support of our position, it was only necessary to say, that we did not admit the right of the belligerent powers to interfere farther in the commerce between neutral nations and their adversaries than to prevent their carrying to them articles, which by common usage were established as contraband, and any articles, to a place fairly blockaded; that consequently the first articles, tho' founded upon their principles of not suffering in a war a traffic, which was not admitted by the same nations in time of peace; and of taking their enemies property when found on board of neutral vessels; were nevertheless countrary to what we contended to be the just principles of the modern law of nations.[39]

Pinckney was searching for assurances of British willingness to amend basic attitudes toward the United States. Grenville replied that the policy had in fact been changed because of the desire to maintain harmonious relations with the United States and the need to remove pretexts causing animosity toward Great Britain. Grenville congratulated Pinckney upon the fair way in which the United States had executed its neutrality policies in American waters and added this as an additional reason for the revocation of the previous Orders in Council.[40] The British Minister believed that under the November 6 orders, cases of seized American ships would be speedily processed by the Admiralty Courts and the new revocation of those orders would free many vessels not yet processed. As an additional concession Grenville promised a reply to Pinckney's protests on the June 8 order, the instruction which had set in motion the divisive developments leading to the rupture between the two powers.[41]

The revocation of the November 6 orders and Lord Grenville's solicitious expressions represented important victories for Pinckney. American and British merchants, immediately aware of the change, attributed them to Pinckney's efforts, and one enthusiastic supporter exclaimed,

I congratulate you on your victory.—I think it augurs a change respecting the trade to Europe, and, of course, the French East Indies.
All stands on one principal; and if it is changed to you, it must be
changed to the other neutral powers. Does it not augur peace also
in due time?[42]

Pinckney modestly denied that his efforts alone had altered
British policy, saying it had been the combination of American merchant protests, the fears of an American war and the
successes of British arms.[43]

In late 1793 Secretary of State Jefferson retired from Washington's Cabinet to be replaced by Edmund Randolph. Yellow
fever and the growing crisis with Great Britain had prevented
Jefferson from answering Pinckney's July, August, and September, 1793 letters. During this time British relations consumed
most of the public debate transpiring in the United States.
Congress, since convening, had focused attention on these relations, and the debates that developed in late 1793 and early
1794 led the United States very close to war. This critical session of Congress ran from December 2, 1793 to June 9, 1794,
and its excessive debating was in reality needless because Lord
Grenville, hoping to preserve peace, began to guide British
policy back toward a more reasonable course. The concessions
which began with the revocation of the November 6 orders included an offer made in early April by the first Lord of the
Admiralty to convoy American vessels in the Mediterranean, a
measure illustrating the lengths to which British efforts at conciliation had gone. That was not the only surprise. Although
maritime regulations to prevent supplies from reaching France
on neutral bottoms were to be rigidly enforced during the
spring campaign, orders went forth from the Admiralty to treat
American vessels and captains with respect. Also, decisions in
the Court of Admiralty began to reflect the new look in British
policy.[44] As early as March, 1794, it was reported that the British Cabinet was seriously considering opening all ports in the
British West Indies to American bottoms and allowing free
importation of all goods.[45]

However, public opinion in the United States remained ignorant of these developments, and retributive measures were debated and adopted by the American Congress. Certainly the early months of 1794 were the most critical for the determination of peace and war between America and Great Britain. Had communications between the officials of the two nations been faster, much of the acrimony and divisiveness of the American debates might have been avoided. For example, not until March 8, 1794 did Pinckney's explosive letter of November 25, 1793 reach Randolph, the new Secretary of State, whose reactions were understandably dramatic. Randolph passed on to members of Congress the information, except for the cyphered sections which, in effect, asked for Pinckney's final recall.[46] As further illustration of the significance of the communications lag, both Washington and Randolph were to remain ignorant of the revocation of the November 6 orders until early April, 1794. Once he had received evidence of the new British approach to negotiations, Washington tried to maintain peace by additional negotiations through John Jay's special mission to London.[47]

Prelude to the
Jay Negotiations

VII

It is now nearly a fortnight, since Mr. Jay was nominated as Envoy Extraordinary to London. The Senate were occupied in this business for some days; objections of various kinds, mingling to interrupt it, such as a supposed inutility of the mission; the sentiments of Mr. Jay upon matters, with which he may be charged, and the constitutional incompatibility or inexpediency of the Chief Justice exercising diplomatic functions. He was confirmed.

—Randolph to Morris, 29 April 1794

THE DEBATE THAT ERUPTED in the United States with the Neutrality Proclamation in 1793 lasted throughout that year and became critical during the early months of 1794. During this first great foreign policy debate in American history, party lines solidified. Subsequent partisan feelings, sometimes shared by historians, have partially obscured the situation as it actually developed.

When the debate opened, four major objections were lodged against Washington's neutral stand: some questioned his constitutional authority to issue such a proclamation; others argued that it violated the treaties with France and that it showed ingratitude to the nation which had aided America in gaining her independence; and still others thought the statement untimely and unnecessary. Alexander Hamilton defended Washington's policy. Hamilton, whose influence was at a high point, was the author of the United States financial system which was built largely upon the income from import duties, tonnage taxes, and internal excise taxes. He argued that the executive right to issue the Proclamation derived from Article II of the Constitution, the clause which empowers the President "to take care that the laws be faithfully executed." Hamilton was a broad constructionist who believed that the power vested in the President was subject only to the exceptions and qualifications specifically expressed in the organic law. To the objections that the Proclamation was contrary to the treaties in force between the United States and France, Hamilton argued that the French Alliance was primarily a defensive one since, according to his interpretation of events, France had attacked England. This fact meant to Hamilton that the terms of the Alliance were therefore no longer technically binding. The young financial genius emphasized that the first duty of any nation is self-preservation, and America was after all without a naval force and France, with the maritime powers allied against her, would be of no help in a war at sea. Thus to ally with France would be the height of folly.[1] Always persuasive in argument, Hamilton made his points effectively. Many of his contemporaries agreed particularly with his analysis of disaster following America's involvement in war. It was a problem of tactics and strategy. Spain and Great Britain had possessions on all sides of the thirteen states, and their control over the Indian tribes in their areas would turn the "interior frontier" into a bloody battleground. With no fortifications, a population of only four million, and no navy, a war with Britain would be disastrous.[2]

Others argued that strong economic ties with Great Britain

offered the best reason and the best hope for eventual settlement of differences. Tench Coxe reminded his countrymen that since the United States was Britain's best market for manufactured goods, British policy would have to recognize American rights, particularly if America emphasized her economic importance by an embargo on all shipping between the two countries for a limited period of time. Exports from the United States in 1793 exceeded twenty-six million dollars, an increase of five million dollars over 1792. Much of this total was made up of exports of wheat and flour, for the demand for these commodities by European belligerents had driven the average price on American markets above one dollar per bushel, greatly benefiting American agriculture.[3]

Great Britain, in fact, furnished America with a greater volume of manufactured goods than did all other foreign nations or colonies combined and Coxe thought that the threat of the loss of such a market would eventually sober British attitudes. Certainly British policy in the Northwest, he believed, was not motivated by economic factors since the Canadian market was vastly inferior to that of the United States and the fur trade constituted only a small proportion of the total Canadian trade. Thus, territorial rather than economic desires guided British policy.[4]

Amid the welter of continuing debate emerged Madison's proposals for new commercial regulations that would retaliate against British violations of American neutral rights. His proposals, introduced into Congress January 3, 1794 at the height of public excitement over British seizures in the West Indies and fresh on the heels of the news of the Algerines being loosed to harass American shipping, attracted much publicity. Although subsequently defeated, the proposals led ultimately to the adoption of embargo measures against Great Britain. The most important provision of Madison's system, however, placed special restrictions and higher duties on the manufactures and navigation of European nations "having no commercial treaty with the United States." Countries denying admission of American produce in American vessels would be given similar treatment in American ports. The economic losses of U.S. citizens occasioned by seizures and the delay resulting from slow judicial procedures would be directly reimbursed to the individuals injured by such actions, from *additional* duties levied on the shipping of the offending nations. This, obviously, was a measure aimed directly at Great Britain.[5]

Madison's proposals were popular, although they were not adopted *in toto*. William L. Smith, a Representative from South Carolina and a personal friend of Pinckney's, attacked the proposals by showing how much more important to the U.S. economy Great Britain was than France. He even went so far as to attack Jefferson's good faith in his negotiations with Hammond. As Smith explained the delay of negotiations, Jefferson insisted upon written documents from the British Government affirming Hammond's powers to negotiate, and when those were not forthcoming, he refused to proceed. Smith commented sneeringly that *"forms* were the obstacle of the Secretary of State, whose zeal, at best, was not greater than Mr. Hammond's."[6] Jefferson's resignation, though, removed him from further criticism and left the Government free to pursue additional measures of accommodation. Such efforts at conciliation, however, would necessarily be made in an atmosphere supercharged with rumor and partisanship.

Such was the situation in the United States when Pinckney's communications arrived containing the "serious intelligence" about British intentions to hold the western posts. His letters, excepting the passages in cypher, were communicated immediately to Congress, and as a result retaliatory measures against Great Britain gained almost universal popularity.[7] Meanwhile, Pinckney impatiently awaited the outcome of the American debates caused by his dispatches. During this period, he regularly filed reports to the State Department on the latest developments in Great Britain detailing changes in British policy as they occurred, although never relaxing his vigilance for American interests. He attended the opening session of Parliament in January, 1794, to hear the King's traditional address. It was clear from that speech and from the ensuing debates in Parliament that Great Britain intended to prosecute the war with France with determination and vigor.

Aware of the controversy raging in America and of his own responsibility for describing European affairs to the State Department, Pinckney summarized the status of European alliances on the eve of the spring military campaigns in Europe. Beginning with Russia, his report covered the entire political map: The Empress of Russia insisted upon complete restoration of the French Monarchy. Sweden remained neutral. Denmark, on the other hand, suffered from seizures by British ships because of the express treaty clauses violated by the British in such actions, but Denmark, nevertheless, remained neutral in the conflict. The Austrian Emperor's finances were exhausted and he had been unable to raise money either in Holland or in Flanders. Likewise, the King of Prussia had depleted his financial resources and was unable to borrow so much as a stiver in Holland. Holland had no independent foreign policy, and despite public opinion, she followed Great Britain's bidding. Portugal, an ally of Spain, contributed little more than stipulated by treaty, and Spain, too, was militarily ineffective. Britain continued to subsidize the King of Sardinia to keep troops on the French frontier. Neutral rights were bravely maintained by Genoa. The French continued to threaten the Mediterranean states, and it appeared that the King of the Two Sicilies would be the first victim of the French. Pinckney felt that the Italian States not yet involved in the conflict would remain neutral as would Switzerland. Poland was merely a province of Russia. The Sublime Porte, it was rumored, was negotiating for British aid to prevent an attack on Turkey by Russia. To Pinckney it was clear that Great Britain was the chief member of the alliance against France. Not only did Britain possess vast pecuniary resources, but she also had eighty battleships, thirty-nine thousand regular troops, and she was raising an additional thirty thousand.

Information gleaned from Americans traveling in France

showed affairs there to be improving. The Republic daily grew in internal strength while external signs of its power were unmistakable. It was reliably reported that France had thirty million sterling in its treasury in gold and silver alone, although she continued to finance her military adventures by issuing assignats.[8]

Thus, Pinckney briefly and expertly detailed the situation among the powers allied against France and contrasted the treatment accorded Americans by the French and by the British, to the detriment of the latter. Although British attitudes had softened and concrete steps were taken to ease the result of the policies of the previous months, American ships continued to be sequestered and sent into British ports under the orders of November 6. In fact, according to a report reprinted in *The Times,* no fewer than thirty-six American vessels lay in British ports seized under the November 6 Orders in Council,[9] even though the original orders had been rescinded. A simple explanation may be that it was almost impossible to contact British ships at sea to give them new instructions. Furthermore, the regular session of the Admiralty Court at which many of these vessels would be judged was scheduled for March 31, and except for special sittings thereafter, the next term would begin on May 5.[10] Thus, legal delays added to and were to continue to increase the difficulties between Britain and the United States.

At this time, Lord Grenville was rewarded for his diplomatic successes with the post of Auditor of the Exchequer. Stocks began rising on the London market with expectations of military victories in the forthcoming spring campaigns.[11]

Serious problems continued to plague Pinckney. He received two anonymous letters signed "your old friend" in early March which informed him that eight or ten Algerian vessels had, with British connivance, put to sea to stop American passenger traffic. They planned to sweep the area bounded by 37° to 39° north latitude and from 33° to 36° west longitude. From Spain Short verified the movement of this fleet into the open sea.[12] Word of the *new* instructions to His Majesty's vessels also reached Pinckney by way of another confidential source, although knowledge of such instructions was denied by Crickitt and Townly, the proctors through whom Pinckney usually procured official information from the Admiralty.

Periodic presses for seamen to man the British fleet continued to take their toll from American sailors, though Pinckney vigorously continued to plead their cause. He again petitioned Grenville for satisfaction on impressment procedures, this time in a very strongly worded note:

Mr. Pinckney cannot avoid on this occasion pressing his regret that Government still declines acceding to permanent arrangements for assuring the security of American seamen in their ports; whereby a nation whose commercial intercourse is of greater importance to Great Britain than that of any other foreign nation, which affords the amplest security to British seamen within its ports; and which has under circumstances of some delicacy manifested the most friendly disposition to this country; continues exposed to what cannot be considered but a grievous calamity.[13]

The continuing seizure of U.S. ships bound to the West Indies kept the American public boiling. Stories circulated that as many as six hundred American vessels were British victims. Although grossly exaggerated, such stories fed the flames of partisanship,[14] knowledge of which Charles Cotesworth Pinckney relayed to his brother in London.[15]

In late March Congress laid a temporary embargo on shipping to Great Britain. Prices of produce on the American market immediately fell and the cost of manufactured goods increased. As one writer complained, "Bad times indeed! produce on hand and none to purchase—and goods twice their value."[16] The efforts at retaliation were not successful nor were they particularly popular, but criticism appeared to be a dangerous thing. It was worth a bloody nose or a black eye, according to "Honestus" in the *National Gazette & Daily Advertiser* of Fredericksburg, Virginia, to say anything opposed to war or embargo. Doubting whether those so disposed toward violent measures really had anything economic at stake, he asked plaintively what the wives and families of working men were to do "in case our commerce should be totally knocked up?"[17]

No sooner were steps taken to implement the embargo in Baltimore, Boston, and other American seaports than Pinckney's letters relating the changed British policy were published in the *National Gazette* and widely reprinted in other American newspapers. This new information (new to the American debate), as well as the deleterious economic effects of the embargo, chastened many in the United States.[18] Others, however, stubbornly continued to demand firm and decisive opposition to Great Britain. Voicing sentiments of outraged nationalism, these individuals thought the neutrality policy nothing but "tame forebearance." The failure to use force against Great Britain had led to their use of even greater force. The United States and Great Britain were, after all, traditional enemies, and the latter had merely waited for an opportunity to avenge her 1776 loss. Embargo of all trade was called for; that is, embargo until reparations for all seizures were made. If the enemy seized ships, seize twice as many in return. The American Executive had been tricked by Machiavellian foreign intrigues. No possible benefit for America *in re* Great Britain existed except the negative one of giving British creditors an annual sum of over six million dollars. No commercial treaty had been signed; western posts were in British hands, and British agents were provoking Indians to attack American settlers in the West; the release of the Algerines to seize American ships in the Mediterranean was but further proof of British treachery. Although the British had by proclamation opened their West Indian ports to U.S. trade, they initiated this move toward conciliation by using special orders to seize all American vessels in that area. Under these provocations there could be no hope of satisfaction. Such were the arguments appearing in United States newspapers in April, 1794.[19]

From his retirement Jefferson observed sentiments among

his countrymen for retaliation against Great Britain and reported to Monroe that the time for firmness had arrived. Unless the Administration did something, and that quickly, the insults to the United States would increase.[20] It was not that he wished war, but that he preferred peace with honor. In reacting to Monroe and Madison's suggestions for a special mission to England headed by Hamilton, Jefferson voiced his political hatred:

A more degrading measure could not have been proposed; and why is Pinckney to be recalled? For it is impossible he should remain there after such a testimony that he is not confided in. I suppose they think him not thorough fraud enough; I suspect too the mission, besides the object of placing the aristocracy of this country under the patronage of that government, has in view that of withdrawing H. from the disgrace & the public execrations which sooner or later must fall on the man who partly by erecting fictitious debt, partly by volunteering in the payment of the debts of others, who could have paid them so much more conveniently themselves, has alienated for ever all our ordinary & easy resources, & will oblige us hereafter to extraordinary ones for every little contingency out of the common line.[21]

Hamilton was not selected, as Jefferson feared he would be. Instead, Washington chose for the assignment Chief Justice John Jay of the Supreme Court. In telling Pinckney of the mission Randolph assured him that the action did not alter his status as Minister Plenipotentiary to the Court of St. James, for Jay would be "Envoy Extraordinary." The Senate confirmed Jay's appointment by a comfortable margin. A final effort to settle differences with Great Britain was to be made. Also, at this time Washington appointed Nathaniel Cabot Higginson as U.S. Commissioner to superintend the filing of appeals in the Admiralty Courts in the British West Indies on behalf of American vessels held captive there,[22] to speed decisions in these Courts, and to smooth over many of the outrages committed by British naval vessels. To some extent these actions mollified public opinion in America, but, as if doubting whether anything positive would come from these measures, a resolution was passed providing for the severance of commercial intercourse with Great Britain should differences not be amicably settled by November 1, 1794. The bill was ordered to be drafted and all classes of Americans settled back to observe the outcome of Jay's use of this threat as an additional means of forcing a settlement with Great Britain.[23]

John Jay's appointment has been viewed by many American historians as an attempt to settle the differences between the two nations by appointing someone sympathetic to the British cause. However, Washington's nomination of Jay may have been motivated primarily by his great respect for his abilities as well as by the slowness of communications. In fact, the actual crisis between the two countries had passed by the time of Jay's arrival in London as a policy of conciliation had already been determined by Grenville and his Ministers partly as a result of Pinckney's actions, protests, and persistence.

At the time of Jay's appointment and before news of it could reach England, Pinckney's popularity with the American merchants in London was at its height. Over two hundred and fifty gentlemen attended a dinner given for Pinckney at the London Tavern the first week of April, 1794. This occasion was enthusiastically reviewed in *The Times:*

The chair was taken by Philip Sansom, Esq. and the day passed with a degree of order, harmony, and conviviality, excelling every thing of the kind we have before witnessed. *The King, Prince of Wales, Queen,* and *Royal Family,* with many other loyal and constitutional toasts were drank; and among other suited to the occasion, *The President of the United States,* was given by the Chairman, who introduced it by an elegant and just compliment to the character of General Washington, which was highly approved and applauded. This was followed by another toast from the Chairman, *Prosperity in the Commerce of Great Britain and America, and Perpetual friendship between the two Countries,* which was received with a burst of applause, expressive of the unanimity and friendship of all the company present.

His Majesty's Ministers were invited, and would have been present, had they not been obliged to attend their levy in both Houses of Parliament.[24]

Even one of Pinckney's schoolmates from pre-Revolutionary days sent him congratulations on the success of his efforts to preserve peace and harmony between the "sons of liberty and old England."[25]

Not only was the United States resentful of Great Britain; Sweden and Denmark, in an effort to halt depredations against their trade, signed a convention in which each agreed to fit out a fleet of eight ships as convoys. (News of this step caused stocks on the London market to fall one percent.)[26] Pinckney was asked by the King of Sweden through his ambassador to St. James whether America wished to join this pact between neutral nations. After acknowledging receipt of the inquiry in the proper diplomatic manner, Pinckney forwarded it to Philadelphia,[27] but as Samuel Flagg Bemis has described it, this scheme for a neutral bloc turned out to be abortive.

It was late in April before news of the debates in America reached the British public whose reaction was one of surprised, almost injured feelings. As *The Times* reported, Congress had "actually debated" whether or not to order reprisals on British ships under the "false supposition that our government had ordered all American ships to be made prizes of." Noting that the question failed passage by two votes and that the correct instructions from the Government were now common knowledge in America, the editors hoped that a reconciliation would follow.[28]

When Washington, finally tiring of Genêt's activities, requested his recall, France asked that Morris also be removed. In a letter explaining this to Morris, Randolph covered the events leading up to Jay's appointment as Envoy Extraordinary to Great Britain.[29] James Monroe replaced Morris in France, but like Genêt, Morris did not return to his native land, at least for many years. According to Channing he roved over Europe as a secret agent for the British Government.[30] At first

Washington contemplated sending Pinckney as Morris' replacement—additional proof of the high regard the nation's Chief Executive held for Pinckney[31]—but as matters turned out, Jay returned to the United States after concluding his mission, Pinckney was ordered to negotiate a treaty with Spain and Rufus King was appointed as Pinckney's successor.

Prospects for peace then brightened everywhere: sentiment in the British Isles was conducive to peace;[32] affairs in Canada were quiet;[33] the effects of the embargo had made it clear to Philadelphians that peace was preferable.[34] And following receipt of the new instructions revoking the November 6 orders in the West Indies, the extremely sensitive Anglo-American situation began to ease.

Attention now swung to the Jay mission to London. Just prior to his departure Randolph explained the reasons for the mission in a letter to Pinckney saying that this was to be a mission of peace and if it failed to unify Americans, it would place the blame for war upon Great Britain. As Randolph described Washington's attitude, he attempted to soften Pinckney's shock at the news of Jay's appointment:

The first, and indeed the principal objection to the appointment of an Envoy arose from a respect for you; it being a maxim with the President to be delicate to every officer of the government. But it was represented to him, that you were too well acquainted with the course of diplomatic business, to feel the smallest dissatisfaction at a measure, the solemnity of which so strongly coincides with the crisis, hanging over us; and which is so customary. Not withstanding this difficulty at length subsided in his mind, he declared expressly in his nomination of Mr. Jay to the Senate, that his confidence in our Minister Plenipotentiary in London continues unchanged; nor would he have selected any character, less than one of the most distinguished, to repair to the Court where you are. He has instructed Mr. Jay to communicate with you without reserve; and to complete the proof of his approbation of your conduct, you are hereby authorized and required, in case Mr. Jay should by death or any extraordinary accident be incapacitated from proceeding in the commissions, given to him, to possess yourself of them, to consider them as addressed to yourself, and to enter upon their execution. Thus will you I trust, be persuaded, that we have not forgotten towards you, what we should have expected for ourselves; and that if any more agreeable style of presenting the subject to the public of yourself could have been devised, we should have seized it with great cordiality.[35]

On May 12, Jay sailed from New York on the *Ohio*. A notice in the New York *Daily Advertiser* caused a crowd of nearly one thousand spectators to assemble to bid him *bon voyage*. They escorted him from Trinity Church to the ship and cheered him lustily three times; as the ship cleared the fort in the harbor, a salute was fired to wish him luck in his attempt to obtain a treaty.[36]

Pinckney and the Jay Treaty

VIII

Mr. Pinckney presents his compliments to Lord Grenville and has the honor of informing 'him that Mr. Jay, who has been appointed by the President of the United States of America therein Envoy Extraordinary to his Britannic Majesty, arrived at Falmouth on the 8th of the present month.

—Pinckney to Grenville, 11 June 1794

WHILE JAY, HIS SON, AND A SECRETARY were bound for England, the embargo on shipping to Great Britain was lifted in the United States and not renewed. In England, the prospects for peace were good. British and American funds on the London exchange were rising because of British friendliness toward America. Although most Englishmen desired peace, its continuance was not a foregone conclusion. Much depended upon the attitude adopted by the Court because, as one writer put it, "the majority of the people of this country (England) are so infatuated in king and court craft, that if we were to quarrel with you without any cause whatever, the war would be strongly supported."[1] Nevertheless, Grenville assured Parliament that his intentions toward the United

States were kindly. He claimed that the treatment given American shipping was preferential as compared to that accorded either Denmark or Sweden. He would not yield, however, the principle that Britain had the right to seize "not for condemnation, but merely to detain, afterwards to value, and then pay for the cargo of ships laden with corn, that were in their voyage for the purpose of supplying the enemy." This principle, he claimed, was supported by the law of nations.[2]

During the next few weeks, Randolph, in an effort to economize his writing, addressed his official correspondence directly to Jay with instructions to pass it on to Pinckney immediately. Since the two men were told to work closely together and since Jay's delicate negotiations depended upon quick communication, it appeared logical to the new Secretary of State, himself inexperienced in his new position, to send all dispatches to Jay, at least while negotiations were under way.

Although news of the altered British policies reached Randolph, his action toward encouraging peaceful public opinion in America was practically nonexistent and events in the United States continued to wear on the nation's patience. Governor Simcoe's move to fortify the rapids of the Miami, Hammond's refusal to consider surrendering the Northwest posts, and the fact that there was no apparent moderation of Admiralty Court harshness in the British West Indies continued to foster anti-British feeling. In fact, public excitement increased so much that Hammond feared for the safety of the British Consuls at Baltimore and Norfolk. It seemed to Randolph that Hammond was searching for pretexts to break off relations with the United States, so believing that the United States should be prepared for every contingency, Randolph reported to his envoys in England that Washington was following Sweden's suggestion that America join the neutrals. According to Randolph, Washington would go further; if Jay's negotiations failed, he would send a minister to Sweden to arrange for participation in the bloc. Thus, Jay was to prepare the neutral representatives for such a possibility, though he was cautioned to proceed delicately with the Swedish Minister who was said to be very friendly with Lord Grenville.[3]

The seriousness of the situation at this particular time can be attested to by the Congressional debates on the raising of an army and whether that army should be a permanent force or mobilized from state militia. Many feared the establishment of a permanent military group whereas others disliked the expense involved in building an army. Preparations for war were continuing on the state level. South Carolina, for example, passed a militia act creating two state divisions and giving the command of one to Charles Cotesworth Pinckney and the other to General Pickens. To Charles war appeared almost inevitable, and he wrote Thomas in London describing preparations in South Carolina: "We are now putting this Harbour in a State of Defense, and to every Battery there is to be a reverberating Furnace for red-Hot Shot," a remark that would evoke memories for Thomas, who had commanded an artillery emplacement on Sullivan's Island in Charleston Harbor during the American Revolution.[4] Other states, too, were calling out their militia and putting their harbors in readiness. In addition to official preparations, democratic societies flourished everywhere. Such groups were a focus for the partisan passions of the time, and though frowned upon by the Government, they were important factors in keeping the public aroused. In activities they resembled the earlier Sons of Liberty.[5]

In an effort to obtain documentation of West Indian ship seizures Jay had asked Randolph to send Samuel Higginson to the islands in order to help Jay and Pinckney resolve the problems caused by British seizure practices. By early June, however, Randolph still had received no word from him, and, as it turned out, Higginson had died of fever shortly after his arrival. Thus was defeated an attempt to establish orderly procedure in the West Indies Admiralty Courts.[6]

Deas returned to London as Pinckney's secretary in June. Arriving shortly before Jay, he immediately set to work freeing

Pinckney to assist Jay in the forthcoming negotiations. From the outset Pinckney cooperated in every possible respect. Although nonplussed at the appointment, Pinckney accepted Jay's mission in good spirit, and Jay in turn reciprocated by explaining that he would in no way supplant Pinckney. He told Pinckney that he had been instructed to communicate all matters to him and to rely upon him for advice and assistance in his negotiations.[7] The evidence in the official files supports the fact that the two men did work in close harmony. Pinckney's pride had suffered a blow, as may be seen in his letter to Randolph after learning of the appointment:

With respect to this gentleman's mission, as it personally concerns me, if I were to say I had not unpleasant feelings on the occasion I should not be sincere; but the sincerity with which I make this declaration will, I trust, entitle me to credit, when I add, that I am convinced of the expediency of adopting any honorable measure, which may tend to avert the calamities of war, or by its failure cement our union at home; that I consider Mr. Jay's appointment, from the solemnity of the mission, supported by his established reputation, diplomatic experience and general talents, as the most probable method of affecting this purpose; and that I am sensible of the delicacy respecting myself with which this measure has been carried into execution. Under these impressions, it will be scarce necessary for me to say further, that I will cheerfully embrace every opportunity of promoting the objects of Mr. Jay's mission and of rendering his residence here agreeable.[8]

Relieved by the testimony of his Government's confidence, relayed to him by Randolph and repeated verbally by Jay, Pinckney thanked Jay for his solicitude and support. In expressing his gratitude for Jay's "friendly manner in which you have communicated the instructions contained in your favor," Pinckney assured him of complete cooperation in the negotiations.[9]

News of Jay's arrival and the purpose of his mission quickly spread through London. The fact that Congress had lifted the embargo, once that move was generally known, greatly improved the chances for a successful negotiation.[10]

Jay set to work immediately. British officials wined and dined him; Pinckney included him in his own official entertaining,[11] assisted him in matters of court etiquette, and introduced him to Lord Grenville. When Jay left America he had no knowledge of the changes which Grenville had already made in the November 6 Orders in Council or of the victories already won by Pinckney in the Court of Admiralty prize cases, but Pinckney briefed Jay on all these developments and emphasized their importance to the new mission. The discrimination in favor of American shipping being practiced in European waters also impressed Jay with the fact that better relations did indeed exist between the two countries.

Jay met with Lord Grenville on June 18, 1794. When first informed of this new attempt to heal the rupture between Great Britain and the United States, many individuals in England hailed Jay's selection enthusiastically. Prior to his arrival British merchants engaged in U.S. trade had conferred with Grenville to smooth the way for negotiations, and they had been assured by him that, provided Jay made no new demands, all differences would be settled amicably.[12] What Grenville must have meant by "new" was over and above the proposals or difficulties already so ably presented to him by Pinckney in earlier conferences. Without a doubt Jay's personality was to be an important factor in the negotiations as Pinckney's had been in the period before them and as Grenville's was to be in the outcome. But personalities notwithstanding, nothing could have been accomplished had not considerations of peace been weighing more heavily than those of war. In a statement at this time Pitt himself promised the Committee of North American Merchants that there truly did exist the same disposition for peace in the American Government as in the British and that there was little doubt in his mind that differences would be settled. Pitt was so optimistic, in fact, that he encouraged them to "execute the orders they now had or might receive."[13]

While matters were developing thus in England, domestic affairs in the United States took a serious turn with the outbreak of the Whiskey Rebellion in western Pennsylvania. Added to the problems of the Indian campaign facing Anthony Wayne and the continuing harassment of American shipping in the Caribbean, this domestic revolt against the excise tax levied on grain-distilled alcohol was viewed by many Americans as another indication of British intrigue. Some even whispered that the British were actively encouraging this resistance to Federal authority. By the end of July a great deal of concern arose over whether British troops were going to assist the Indians against Wayne, and the seriousness of the "tumult near Pittsburg" had not yet been determined.[14]

In any case, domestic events such as the yellow fever epidemic and the Whiskey Rebellion served to concentrate the attention of U.S. officials on home affairs to the momentary detriment of foreign matters. Nowhere did it hurt more than in the poor communications maintained by the State Department with American representatives abroad. Pinckney, of course, received no correspondence from Jefferson during the course of the yellow fever outbreak, and the information he did receive was usually quite old. William Short in Spain was amazed at Pinckney's scanty information on American affairs although he himself gleaned much current news from Spanish mercantile houses. But he, too, complained to Pinckney of the Department's failure to keep its foreign officers informed when in June he wrote bitterly that "other countries think it necessary to keep their foreign ministers well informed & with speed & regularity." He believed it better for countries not to keep representatives abroad rather than that they be "kept without such information."[15] Here was Short, Jefferson's private secretary, complaining of the performance of Randolph, his friend and successor, in a most helpless manner:

When I reflect on the circumstances in which we were placed I know not how to believe my own experience of such neglect—I expect no change in the system, so completely seems it to have been established in the department of foreign affairs.[16]

While internal developments held the attention of Washington and his Cabinet, the American people hung on to the latest foreign news. One article from the *Minerva* reprinted in the *National Gazette* exclaimed that it had been at least ten days since it had received any "bloody" news from Europe. Coffee houses were dull, for appetites whetted by news of thousands of deaths were not to be satisfied with coverage of local events.[17] The sentiment for war continued strong in the country, particularly in the South where the French cause had always been popular.[18]

In London Pinckney carried on his routine duties, protesting the burning of the American ship *Rambler* and demanding compensation from the British Government,[19] passing along the news of Jay's arrival to David Humphreys in Lisbon and Short in Madrid,[20] and protesting the detention of some French passengers taken by the British from an American ship.[21] During the negotiations between Jay and Grenville, he never relaxed his pressure on the British Government to deal justly with American shipping and to cease its abhorrent impressment practices. On July 5, he demanded Grenville's attention to the problems caused by British detention of American vessels, for although it was true that captured American ships had been released after their captains were paid for cargoes and freight, they still could not sail owing to their "want of money to pay their expenses incurred during their detention here, as on account of the length of time which [was] occupied in passing their accounts." Pinckney felt that it would help if prompt payment according to the decrees of the Court of Admiralty could be made to such individuals.[22] On the very next day he protested the impressment of American sailors from the *William Penn*, all of whom were under the American Consul's protection.[23]

For the summer Pinckney sent his son and daughters to a cottage at Leatherhead, Surrey, under the care of a governess. He and his wife, Betsey, visited them from time to time, but such extravagances added to the costs of maintaining his mission for his salary did not cover his expenses. To defray living costs, he had rice sent from his South Carolina plantation. He sold these cargoes for good prices in the British market and used the proceeds to supplement his diplomat's salary.[24]

Pinckney also spent the summer aiding Lafayette. By an act of Congress passed on March 27, 1794, a transfer of credit exceeding twenty-four thousand dollars for back pay and allowances was made to Lafayette. An agent from America, James Marshall, the younger brother of John Marshall, was sent to Berlin as a special emissary to obtain the intercession of that Court on Lafayette's behalf. Marshall's attempts, however, failed. Lafayette was removed to the Austrian fortress of Olmutz in Moravia, and Pinckney contented himself with forwarding a letter to Lafayette in which he told him of the money voted him by a grateful American Congress.[25]

In deference to Jay's efforts in negotiation and in order to avoid jeopardizing the mission, Pinckney began to clear his protests with Jay before presenting them to Grenville.[26] Such was the case when Pinckney applied for the relief of six seamen impressed in the West Indies and brought by prison ship to England. As he explained it, their sudden seizure had prevented them from bringing papers to prove their identity, but the American Consul in London remembered the men having had papers on previous voyages. Pinckney, however, requested Grenville's interposition on their behalf, noting that his intervention in impressment cases was not having the effect it once had.[27]

Meanwhile, both Pinckney and Jay continued to be fêted by members of the British Cabinet—certainly a great change from the early days of the mission when Pinckney was continually ignored by British officialdom. (Late in July they even dined with the Duke of Portland.)[28]

While observing negotiations and advising Jay when asked, Pinckney further occupied himself by endeavoring to brief Short, in Spain, on developments in America and northern

Europe. To him he described the vigorous exertions being made in the United States for defense: the militia was in a state of readiness, eighty thousand were on call; one corps of engineers and two corps of artillery had been added to the regular force, making about one thousand men; and appropriations on frigates had been passed in Congress and the captains had been selected. It might be added that the frigates were intended for defense against the Algerians and it was Pinckney's duty to purchase copper (for sheathing their bottoms) and other equipment for them from Great Britain. Thus, at the height of Jay's negotiations, Pinckney was asking the British Government for permission to export from England equipment for finishing six frigates that could be used against Great Britain, should negotiations fail.[29] However, Pinckney was to receive the permission without objection.

News of Jay's successful arrival and of his cordial reception reached America in early July and delighted the Chief Executive, though public opinion was still anti-British. One particular incident at this time alarmed Hammond, who in these rather tense days showed less diplomatic poise than previously. A French vessel, *L'Amiable Gentille*, which had been granted release to "proceed in ballast" from an American port, was found, when intercepted by a British frigate, to be loaded with one hundred and fifty barrels of powder.[30] Hammond's reactions were violent. Randolph, in recounting the episode to Jay, said that he was grateful that nations did not permit themselves to construct their foreign policies upon the recommendations of their envoys alone.[31] Randolph, himself excited, resurrected for Jay every charge against the British that was even being rumored in America. He felt that Simcoe's invasion of the rapids of the Miami alone was reason enough to blame the deterioration of relations solely upon British machinations.[32]

In the West Indies the British fleet lay immobilized by yellow fever, and the British residing there accused Americans of poisoning the flour and other provisions imported into the islands since the lifting of the embargo. By mid-July these accusations dissipated, and all British interference with American shipping stopped. Now, in fact, "every possible protection is given to American vessels, by the men of war, and the Revenue officers."[33] It had required six months for the January 8, 1794 orders to become effective in the West Indies—another example of the slowness of communication.

Slowly but surely the policy of reason and arbitration appeared to be winning. Soothing letters now appeared with greater frequency in American newspapers, many of which hailed the wisdom of America's neutrality.[34] It was at this time that personal tragedy struck Pinckney. His wife, Betsey, whom he loved devotedly, died in August, 1794. Grief-stricken, he fled to the country with his children, leaving his affairs in the hands of his secretary. In his absence Deas handled the mission's affairs.

While Pinckney mourned, false news of a treaty with Great Britain reached New York. It was published in the Philadelphia *National Gazette* and subsequently spread throughout the country.[35] And within a few weeks of each other, the Whiskey Rebellion was suppressed and the Indian threat in the Northwest ended by Wayne's victory at Fallen Timbers. Randolph opened negotiations with Spain for free navigation of the Mississippi and ordered Humphreys from Lisbon to Algiers to ransom American captives there and to effect a truce with the Algerines.[36] Thus, the United States began to extricate itself from some of its most troublesome problems.

Returning to his duties on September 15, Pinckney announced to Randolph that the British Government had revoked the instruction "authorizing their ships of war to stop and detain all vessels bound with corn meal and flour to the dominions of France." Victory belonged to the American cause at last. The principle for which Pinckney had so long contended was now acknowledged by Grenville, at least until a treaty was completed and ratified. Undoubtedly Grenville calculated that this revocation would calm American tempers already roused by British policies and aid in the ratification of the treaty. The negotiations themselves moved slowly. Pinckney's deep involvement is proved by his descriptions of them to Randolph:

of the final event thereof it is yet impossible to decide with certainty. Indeed it is not surprising when parties differ so widely, on various points of discussion, that there should be considerab'e difficulty in removing their reciprocal objections. It is however, evident that present appearances offer a reasonable hope, that a more favourable *composition* of our differences may take place than was some time ago within the scope of my expectation.[37]

Grenville's decision to treat France-bound neutral vessels more leniently until a final settlement was heartily approved by Washington and Randolph. Since Jay lacked lists of ships captured in the West Indies, Randolph desired that Jay not be put off in his negotiations by Grenville's demand to see the case files of captured ships. Jay was to defend the principle involved and not to rest his case on the inaccurate and incomplete examples of seizures in the possession of American officials. He should not argue specific cases on their individual merits. It was Washington's wish that Jay not push negotiations "beyond the dictates of prudence." He was to be guided by circumstances, to be conciliatory, but he was not to become a victim of British "finesse and chicane." It was clear that if these attempts at peace failed, the blame was to fall upon the British.[38] The negotiations dragged into November, five months from their commencement, and Jay's concessions to British demands grew greater. Throughout the discussions Jay proved to be more poorly informed about America's domestic affairs than his opponent, a source of constant embarrassment.[39]

While these negotiations were dragging to a climax in London, Washington decided to send an envoy extraordinary to Spain to complete the negotiations there on the Mississippi boundary and navigation question. After carefully considering a number of candidates for this most delicate mission, the

Chief Executive chose Thomas Pinckney, not only because of his faithful and excellent service at the Court of St. James, but because he was most anxious to assuage feelings slightly ruffled by Jay's appointment. Navigation of the Mississippi, rights which were being denied to western settlers, loomed as one of the most important problems of the moment, and it could be obtained only by negotiation with Spain, who exercised jurisdiction over New Orleans and the outlet to the sea. Randolph, in a dispatch dated November 3, informed Pinckney of his new mission which was not, in any way, to interfere with his position as Minister Plenipotentiary to St. James.[40]

Pinckney did not receive official notice of his selection for these new negotiations until mid-February, 1795. But before receiving word, he could report officially the conclusion of the Jay negotiations and claim some credit for his work on the Jay Treaty:

Mr. Jay has communicated freely with me on this subject during the course of the negotiation and I have witnessed the great difficulties, which have occured in adjusting some of the Articles. Although some points might have been arranged more beneficially for us if the treaty had been dictated entirely by the United States; yet when it is considered, as a composition of differences where mutual complaints had rendered mutual concessions necessary to establish a good understanding, I think it may fairly be said, that as little has been conceded by Mr. Jay and as much obtained for the United States as all circumstances considered could be expected. The business upon the whole has been concluded more beneficially for us than I had any hope we could obtain by negotiation six months ago, and in my opinion places us in a more advantageous situation than we should have been by becoming parties to the war.[41]

Pinckney requested that a special agent be sent at once to London to speed the appeals for the cases of American citizens, and this appeal, supported by Jay, resulted in the selection of Samuel Bayard to handle the matters before the British Admiralty Court.[42] For the next several months the diplomatic problem at the Court of St. James was to be concerned primarily with claims and suits in the Admiralty Courts, though suspense would remain high while the Jay Treaty was debated in America and until final ratifications of the Treaty were exchanged.[43]

Pinckney has never received proper acknowledgment for his assistance in helping to devise the Jay Treaty. This is singular indeed, since Jay himself willingly admitted his debt to the South Carolinian:

> I ought not to omit mentioning the acknowledgements due from me to Mr. Pinckney, with whom I have every reason to be satisfied, and from whose advice and opinions I have derived light and advantage in the course of the negotiations. His approbation of the treaty gives me pleasure, not merely because his opinion corresponds with my own, but also from the sentiments I entertain of his judgment and candor.[44]

From the beginning of his mission Pinckney had maintained pressure on the British Government. At one point, in 1793, he had been willing to break off diplomatic relations with Great Britain. His continued and numerous protests over impressment and ship seizures during his mission and the subsequent yielding of the British Foreign Office prepared the way for Jay's negotiation. When Jay arrived, Pinckney served as his adviser, and in this capacity he was invaluable. While American partisans in the debates over the Treaty would view it as a shameful document, British statesmen were later to condemn it. When speaking of the Treaty in 1812, Lord Sheffield commented that with the outbreak of that war, "We have now a complete opportunity of getting rid of that most impolitic treaty of 1794, when Lord Grenville was so perfectly duped by Jay."[45]

This attitude of both British and Americans strongly suggests that the Jay Treaty was doomed to become infamous, whatever merits it might have possessed.

A Final Determination

IX

this Court for its own honor & the honor of the nation was bound to render justice to these sufferers—which if it neglected or refused doing it shared the approbium—and countenanced the injustice of the captors—of men who would most probably have involved this country in another war with America had it not been for the great moderation of its Executive Government.

—A British Judge of the Admiralty Court, May, 1796

HIS MISSION ACCOMPLISHED, Jay and his entourage returned to the United States late in May, 1795. They arrived just in time to observe the great partisan debates over ratification of the Jay Treaty, although months of doubt and uncertainty remained before final ratifications of the Treaty were exchanged. In fact, Pinckney began and completed his Spanish negotiations during the course of this dispute in America.

In May Pinckney completed his preparations for the Spanish mission. He lodged the smaller children with the Monroes in Paris, leaving his son, Thomas, in London with William Allen Deas, who was to act in Pinckney's stead during his absence. After paying his official respects to Lord Grenville, which

resulted in a much warmer meeting than in the months immediately past, Pinckney left London on May 11, 1795 for Paris,
then to Bayonne in southern France, and on to Madrid.[1] The
journey and the various stops along the way consumed forty-
eight slow, tedious and uneventful days. He found Paris a
scene of political anarchy, watching affairs from behind the
shutters of the Monroe residence. He did report to Randolph
that although grain appeared to be in short supply, the coun-
tryside promised a bountiful harvest.[2] Finally, after paying the
exhorbitant bribes necessary to obtain passports, Pinckney and
his party averaged fifty miles per day to the Spanish border,
though they sometimes had to depend on oxen for motive
power.[3] He reached Madrid on June 29, 1795; by the first week
of July he had completed his presentation ceremonies at Court
and begun the negotiations that were to end successfully within
four months.[4] As he had proved in the trying London mission
days, Pinckney was not a man to procrastinate.

The story of the Madrid negotiations, fascinating in its own
right, has been ably recounted by Samuel Flagg Bemis in his
Pinckney's Treaty. Those negotiations are not germane to
Pinckney's London mission except to underscore the fact that
he possessed a high degree of diplomatic skill.[5]

Pinckney followed developments in London through constant correspondence with Deas. He learned that Randolph
had instructed Deas to protest British measures, but lacking the
skill of his superior, Deas proved intemperate in language and
infuriated the British.[6] The extent to which Randolph mud-
died diplomatic waters by his own poorly worded instructions,
made more serious perhaps by Deas' inexperience, can only be
estimated in light of Randolph's subsequent pro-French activities. Certainly his ramrod-like attitude at this very critical time
exacerbated Anglo-American relations.

In London affairs continued to press upon Deas; no relaxa-
tion followed the successful initial phase of treaty negotiations.
Samuel Bayard, sent to represent American interests in British
Admiralty Courts with the expectation of speeding up proce-

dures, soon became the key figure in working out a final under-standing with Great Britain on neutral rights. His problem was gigantic. He discovered the number of actual cases pending in the Courts to be greater than the three hundred estimated by Randolph, and to complicate matters each case apparently had to be considered on its individual merits. Speedy decisions could not be expected, Bayard reported to Randolph, because there were too many interested parties who desired extended litigation, profiting from condemnation. Furthermore, so many other things could happen to render evidence of ownership technically defective that, once cases were brought to trial, restitution might prove difficult. In addition, most captures being tried were those made by privateers in the West Indies, the seat of adjudication having been shifted from the Islands to the London Admiralty Courts. (Many West Indian captures were made after the revocation of the November 8 Orders in Council.) Bayard had to deal with only sixty cases of capture by ships of the British navy owing to Pinckney's foresight, for before departing for Spain, he had assisted Bayard in reaching an agreement with Sir William Scott on methods for handling the cases of American vessels and cargoes captured by West Indian privateers. Final judgment was to be suspended, in many instances, until papers from American claimants reached English Admiralty Courts—a considerable concession in view of previous practices.[7] While Pinckney negotiated in Spain, Bayard labored to establish a system for the settlement of American ship seizures. It was in this particular area that peace was finally established. Work went steadily forward despite the absence of a coordinated policy in the British Administration and echoes of dissent coming from America on the Jay Treaty. As Bayard received additional papers on spoliations from the United States, he initiated the legal processes leading to final judgments. He encountered unexpected difficulties such as high court costs and complex filing procedures. Nevertheless, real progress toward the establishment of a working system appeared by early May.[8]

The situation was too complex, however, to expect an easy

and smooth settlement. In a momentary flurry tempers were to flare again and a short, sharp crisis was to test the strength of the new understanding between Great Britain and the United States. Fortunately for both countries, the Jay Treaty would meet its test, and peace, for the moment, was to be realized.

At this juncture, however, the British navy, under unpublished orders, again began capturing American ships carrying grain to France. It did this under an article in the Jay Treaty which recognized the ancient "law of nations" stating that belligerents had the right to confiscate enemy property in neutral bottoms.[9] Grain was again scarce in England. Americans, believing their problems solved, were naturally exasperated, although Deas and Bayard worked around the clock to allay resentments and to explain the situation as best they could. The only bright spot in an otherwise dismal picture was the increased British effort to speed the latest captures to quick adjudication. As soon as the vessels reached port, their papers and the master and crew interrogations were forwarded to the Courts of Admiralty in London where they were immediately inspected and laid before the King's advocate without delay. The vessels, if the lawful property of U.S. citizens, were released immediately, whereas their cargoes were confiscated but paid for by the British Government—a margin of ten percent profit being permitted the owners. Payments were made, however, only to those owners who filed legal claims for the goods. These efforts to speed procedures were attempts to forestall the outrage of American merchants whose patience had already been pushed to its limits. Despite good intentions, the large number of cases overloaded the flimsy machinery of justice, and the inevitable delays occurred.[10] Deas' responses to these events were faithful to Randolph's instructions. He peppered the British Ministry with his protests while reporting to Pinckney the resumption of the seizures.[11] At first Deas told Grenville that American merchants were inclined to accept the system if payment for cargoes were quickly made,[12] but as delays increased, so did Deas' impatience,[13] as he experienced a series of

episodes similar to those Pinckney encountered before the revocation of the November, 1793 Orders in Council. To Deas,
at least, the crisis seemed equally severe.

The novice diplomat seized every opportunity to complain
and kept up an annoying chatter of objections that irritated
Lord Grenville and so alarmed State Department officials that
they were finally forced to give Deas a stern lecture on proper
diplomatic language. Between July, 1795 and January, 1796
Deas addressed twenty-five notes to Grenville protesting British
conduct, but lacking Pinckney's advice and out of touch with
developments in the United States, he overreacted to British
actions.[14] When answers to his protests were not forthcoming,
he jogged Grenville by issuing a deadline for a response.[15]
Furthermore, he grew discontented with the arrangements for
the payment of confiscated cargoes, for it seems that the rise in
grain prices made the ten percent profit margin no longer
attractive. Deas suggested as an alternative that prices be set
according to the market and in relation to the expense of the
individual voyage and not, as they were currently, by a blanket
rate.[16] Grenville's studied silence enraged Deas, who threatened
Grenville.[17] Although he reviewed grievances (British cruisers
and crews had "violated" American commerce, "impressed"
American citizens, and "abused" passengers on American vessels), the British Minister refused to answer his formal notes of
protest. To Deas there was nothing in such conduct promising
reconciliation or friendship. If the British were silently waiting
for news of the success or failure of the Jay Treaty, then their
reticence was even more inexcusable.[18] Ratification, though, of
the Treaty was uncertain, and British excesses would not speed
its passage. Deas hoped that its final ratification would intro-
duce a new era of harmony in the relations of the two countries, but should the Treaty fall "and it be necessary to resort
to hostile measures let the impartial world judge between the
U.S. and Great Britain at whose door the aggression and its
consequences must be laid."[19]

Deas had gone too far. Lord Grenville stated that the points raised by Deas were, in reality, already settled by the Treaty and that he had been acting on the assumption that the Treaty would be ratified. Shocked by Grenville's sternness, Deas tried cajolery, but claimed his right to report violations against his country's interests.[20] However, he did temper his tone in future messages to Grenville, although he continued to remind him of the effect such incidents were having "on the executive and the people at large of the United States under the existing circumstances."[21] By mid-September Deas had apologized to Grenville for his intemperance.[22]

Not until the arrival of an official letter dated August 25, 1795 from Timothy Pickering, Randolph's successor as Secretary of State, did Pinckney learn that the Jay Treaty had finally been ratified and Randolph had resigned.[23] Earlier letters from Deas had merely reported public reactions to the Jay Treaty in Great Britain and America.[24]

Pickering, the third Secretary of State during the Pinckney mission, ordered John Quincy Adams from The Hague to London to handle the formal exchange of treaty ratifications.[25] The fact that in such a short time it was necessary for Washington to appoint three Secretaries of State testifies to the confusion of this period in American history.

In the United States controversy raged over Randolph's dismissal and the Jay Treaty; in England the arrival of the Treaty and the need to hurry its final approval coincided with a particularly tense time. One moment it looked as if the Treaty would fail and hostilities would break out; the next, all was peaceful, and real efforts to compromise began to appear. By early September the last crisis prior to the final exchange of ratifications was past. Orders went out to British vessels to stop detaining neutral vessels to French ports.[26] It remained, however, a problem for Bayard, Deas, and Pinckney to arrange a suitable method for quick compensation to American owners for the seizures already suffered.[27]

As his negotiations in Spain neared completion, Pinckney

asked Washington for his recall. He gave ample notice—until June, 1796. Four years of foreign service were enough. He could no longer afford the personal expense and his family, now motherless, needed his attention. He apologized to Washington for any embarrassment caused him in the controversy over the Jay Treaty since he had been responsible for much of its formulation.[28]

As Washington explained to Pinckney, the course of the Treaty in the United States had not been a smooth one. Indeed, it had caused the greatest public excitement since the American Revolution.[29] The Chief Executive himself had disliked the Treaty when he received it and therefore delayed presenting it to the Senate. It passed the Senate with great difficulty and even after it had done so, Washington still hesitated to sign it. At this point, through Hammond, there came to Washington's attention documents implicating Randolph with the French diplomat, Fauchet, in an attempt to sway important Americans to the French cause. Washington abruptly dismissed Randolph, and the cry against the Treaty became blurred by the personal struggle between Randolph and Washington.[30]

News that Pinckney firmly supported the Treaty was questioned by several, but Charles Cotesworth Pinckney spread the word that his brother in fact did give the Treaty his wholehearted support.[31] Thus, after much bickering, doubt, and indecision the Jay Treaty was finally approved, signed, and ratified.

It now remained principally to Bayard to make peace a reality. Though doubting the fairness of the Admiralty Courts,[32] he began his task with enthusiasm, attempting to settle as many cases as possible before turning them over to the United States/British Commissioners provided for in the Jay Treaty. And in fact, the Courts of Admiralty and Appeals, as if to underline his fears, adjourned until November 4. Early in September Bayard noted the suspension of the summer crisis when he announced to Pickering that "The orders for sending in American and other neutral vessels laden with provisions have this day been revoked."[33] Although ship captures in British waters ceased immediately, Bayard continued to represent the American cause at the "Cockpit." George Hammond, British Minister to the United States, returned to London in October bearing a copy of the Jay Treaty signed by President Washington.[34] The ratifications were exchanged and British attitudes immediately improved. By the end of December, on the eve of Pinckney's return to London from his successful Spanish mission, Bayard observed a marked improvement in British actions and attitudes in the Admiralty Courts. Undoubtedly the American delays in signing and ratifying the Jay Treaty accounted for much of this.

To the very end of his overseas missions Pinckney was troubled by the continuous breakdown of communications. In Paris, in December, on his return from Madrid he heard of Adams' removal to London. Since nothing concerning this appointment had reached Pinckney, he at first thought that he had been replaced by Adams, and although understandably disappointed, he swallowed his pride and continued to London, hoping that his experience would be of assistance to Adams as it had been to Jay.[35] But by the time Pinckney returned to London on January 15, 1796, and discovered that he still held his position, the last crisis between the two nations had passed, and Commissioners were being selected to settle ship claims.

Despite the apparent seriousness of British disregard for American neutral rights throughout the crisis from 1792 to 1796, the United States consistently held to its neutrality, absorbing all provocations by the British. To Washington and Pickering loss of pride in the court of nations was preferable to the destruction of the young Republic. However hard it was to make the choice, they found themselves restraining their representatives to the Court of St. James. Or, as Pickering candidly explained to Monroe, while Americans in Paris were embarrassed by the Jay Treaty, British domination of the seas would have permitted England, in the event of war, to destroy the American merchant marine in one year. Likewise, American agriculture would have suffered a terrible blow. Public credit would have been destroyed, and commerce would have failed. Poverty and misery would have resulted, and France would not have received *any* form of aid with American harbors under British siege. This was the reason Washington and his Secretaries of State chose to remain neutral. It was a policy justifiable solely by considerations of survival.[36] Such observations echoed those Jefferson made as early as 1793.

Pinckney's return relieved Deas of responsibilities beyond his diplomatic ability, and Bayard greeted him enthusiastically, saying that his appearance would have "an auspicious influence on the business of the claims and appeals."[37] Others joined him in greeting Pinckney.[38] He quickly thrust himself into his duties: he attended hearings on ships' claims with Bayard at the "Cockpit" almost before unpacking,[39] made several tentative appointments with Grenville, finally obtaining an audience in late January at which he paid his official respects, took over from Adams all responsibility for claims settlements and became the contact with Grenville through which were made final arrangements of the principles upon which the various classes of American cases were to be based.[40] In addition to his representations to the British Government on behalf of American claimants, Pinckney hoped to continue negotiations on suspended Article 12 of the Jay Treaty, which regulated the tonnage of vessels trading between the United States and the British West Indies. (This Article, the most unpopular, was not approved during the acceptance of the Treaty in America.) Although Adams had originally been given this assignment, Pinckney, who had been a party to the original proceeding, thought he should undertake the final negotiations. He still believed the original Treaty was a positive achievement.[41] However, instructions from Pickering on these additional negotiations did not arrive before Pinckney's return to the United States.

After months of delay, hostility, and refusal to act, the Admiralty Courts in March, 1796 issued a series of far-reaching decisions which finally settled the neutral shipping problem. Bayard hailed the decisions as the victory they really were for American rights and the result for which Pinckney had so long and faithfully contended. The first series of such issues decided were the "Martinique" cases dealing with vessels taken by British forces in the West Indies. In one instance the judge upbraided the captors and restored the vessel and its cargo to their owners, together with full costs and damages. At other times, the Court returned vessels and cargoes without costs and damages, leaving Bayard to appeal these particular decisions.[42] Pinckney protested these last obstructions to Grenville, but all the claims soon passed into the hands of the Commissioners under the Jay Treaty.[43] Whatever delays remained were technical or juridical ones. The American cause had won its final victory. Eventually American merchants would receive full compensation for illegal captures of their ships and cargoes. This was Pinckney's personal triumph, but overreaching this was the fact that peace had been maintained. Pinckney's long and serious efforts had finally met with success.[44]

End of a Successful Mission

X

*History has unfortunately so many examples of the rarest merit and
most imminent services ill requited. . . .*

—*Pinckney to Washington, May 1796*

PINCKNEY NOW BEGAN impatiently counting the days until his
release from official duties. To Jefferson he wrote longingly
that he too would soon be enjoying agricultural pursuits far
from the "acrimonious extremes to which party matters appear
to have been carried in our country," unaware that he was
addressing the leader of the Anti-Federalists.[1]

As he turned to his final chores of office, Pinckney attempted
unsuccessfully to have Deas made permanent secretary of the
American legation in London, but Deas' recent diplomatic
indiscretions defeated him.[2] Then, Pinckney completed the
ticklish arrangements for furnishing Humphreys with money
to carry the treaty with Algeria into effect, sent copies of the
Jay Treaty to President Washington, and continued his representations for U.S. citizens to Lord Grenville. From afar he
listened to the post-approval arguments in the United States
over the Jay Treaty. There, resentment over the Treaty con-

tinued unchecked, and so unhappy with the results of its passage were some members of Congress that they demanded to see a copy of Jay's instructions before approving funds with which to make the Treaty effective. In this political and constitutional battle, Washington was forced to muster all his forces to obtain a victory which cost him popularity. Never in his entire career was that Chief Executive so violently and bitterly attacked. Only by using the dread of war did the Administration manage to stave off a defeat.[3]

Once this constitutional crisis had passed, Pinckney's Spanish Treaty was unanimously and quickly ratified. Humphreys was made Minister to Spain, Christopher Gore and William Pinckney were chosen Commissioners to Great Britain under the terms of the Jay Treaty and Rufus King relinquished his Senate seat for Pinckney's position at the Court of St. James.[4]

Pinckney's popularity in the United States, following the unanimous approval of the Treaty with Spain, was at its height. Newspaper editors, still concerned by recent debates over the Jay Treaty, compared the two, the advantage consistently falling to the Pinckney Treaty. In the Spanish Treaty the United States had obtained all it asked for without a single concession, whereas in the "infamous British Treaty," one editor wrote furiously, "all is sacrificed—not an advantage is secured without the basest surrender of the most important rights." To many Pinckney had proved himself the superior diplomat, for Jay had spent three years in Spain trying to negotiate a treaty which Pinckney completed in less than two months![5] As unfair as these observations were to Jay, they represented the thinking of a large number of Americans in 1796, for few people stopped to consider the entirely different situations confronting the two. None knew of Pinckney's assistance to Jay, and most refused to believe, even after it was repeatedly reported that Pinckney supported the Jay Treaty, that he truly did so.[6]

The praise now falling on Pinckney's ears was most welcome. It came from all levels of American society. Washington broke a long silence especially to commend him in a personal note of thanks. Forgotten now were Washington's impatient outbursts over Pinckney's failure to inform him of the progress of his Spanish mission. The success of the Treaty completely thawed Washington's attitude.[7] Final exchanges of ratifications of the Pinckney Treaty occurred in Madrid on May 9, 1796, exactly two months after Washington declared the Jay Treaty in full effect despite the failure of the ratified copy of the Treaty to arrive in the United States.[8]

Meanwhile, Pinckney postponed his plans for a summer return to the United States. While waiting for word of his replacement, he busied himself with routine mission affairs, proving himself a hard worker to the end. Following his successful arrangements for the orderly settlement of claims by American merchants in the Courts of Admiralty, Pinckney made one valiant last effort to establish a permanent procedure for the settlement of impressment cases. Asking the Consuls under his direction to give him all the evidence of citizenship for persons held by the British, he flooded Grenville's desk with requests for the release of the Americans. All in all he filed fourteen firmly worded appeals during a three-month period.[9] Pinckney's hopes for some permanent solution to this problem, however, were doomed to disappointment, for in fact, the British continued to impress American seamen, as crises demanded, until the War of 1812.

As already indicated, it had been Pickering's intention to have Pinckney negotiate the suspended Article 12 of the Jay Treaty, but the long delays consumed by congressional debates over funds for the Treaty caused him to give this assignment to Pinckney's successor, Rufus King.[10] As he awaited the arrival of his successor and of the Jay Treaty Commissioners, Pinckney, after closing out the official financial affairs of both his missions, exulted in a letter to Pickering:

I have received much satisfaction from the accounts lately received of the termination of the business in the House of Representatives relating to the British treaty and it is now to be hoped that matters will go more smoothly between the two countries.[11]

He was pleased to see peace between Great Britain and the United States become a reality, for he had contributed a large part in its establishment at great personal sacrifice. He had lost his wife. His expenses had been enormous. In one year alone, for example, his expenditures exceeded his income by three thousand dollars, a considerable sum in the 1790's. His plantation, having been under the general direction of his brother, needed his personal attention and rebuilding just as did his fortune.[12]

Gore was the first of the Jay Treaty Commissioners to arrive in London and Pinckney quickly arranged for his presentation to British officials.[13] Rufus King sailed from New York on June 20 and arrived in London one month later. Pinckney greeted him with enthusiasm, helped him settle into adequate quarters, arranged for his presentation at Court,[14] and sent a circular letter to the American Consuls in the British Isles announcing the arrival of his replacement.[15] This notice and the formal presentation of his successor to the Court completed Pinckney's responsibilities as Minister Plenipotentiary to the Court of St. James. Presenting his letter of recall to the Court in his last appearance there, the King asked him

to inform the government of the United States that he would punctually comply with the stipulations of the treaty he had lately entered into with them; that he always made a point of fulfilling his engagements which he believed was more than the United States would find executed by other powers with whom they have treaties.[16]

This was to prove a prophetic statement, for France, incensed at the Jay Treaty and involved in internal political chaos, was soon to begin preying on American ships almost as retaliation for the agreement between America and Great Britain. Pinckney's mission to London was done. August was spent in preparation for his return to the United States.[17]

Early in October the Pinckney family began its homeward voyage. Upon his arrival, Pinckney found himself a candidate for the United States Presidency, a bid that proved unsuccessful when John Adams won the nomination by a narrow margin. This was but one sign of the high esteem in which his countrymen held him,[18] for today Pinckney can be said to have been a member of the "establishment." Serving under Washington and Jefferson and alongside Adams and Monroe, Pinckney's acquaintances included many illustrious men of the time. Despite his announced wish to retire to his plantation, Pinckney was elected by his fellow South Carolinians to a two-year term in Congress from which, for reasons of health, he retired in 1798. From that time until the War of 1812 and then during the remainder of his life, he devoted his time to his family and rebuilding his estates. During the War of 1812 he was commanding general of the Southern Department.

Shortly after his return to the United States, Pinckney paid his respects to Washington,[19] who congratulated Pinckney for his long and loyal service to the nation. As Washington plaintively observed,

To receive testimonies of this kind from the good and virtuous, more especially from those who are competent to judge, and have had the means of judging from the best sources of information, stamps a value which renders it peculiarly grateful to one's sensibility.[20]

Reiterating his reasons for holding firmly to neutrality, Washington described the partisanship that was developing in American domestic affairs wondering "who are true Americans, those who are stimulating a foreign nation to unfriendly acts, repugnant to our rights and dignity?" Pinckney, like Washington, to the end of his public career held firmly to the policy of neutrality. He believed that the XYZ Affair and the subsequent quick change of public opinion to the support of Washington's position finally verified the wisdom of neutrality.[21] He was happy in May, 1798 to congratulate Washington on "the change of sentiment effected by recent events on the public mind relating to our foreign connections."[22] In a fine philosophical frame of mind, he told Washington:

After all I can not think it dishonorable to the American character to have been reluctant to war,—to have cherished the remembrance of just services with uncommon fervor & to have been hurried very far by zeal in favor even of the semblance of republican liberty.

If artful men have availed themselves of these dispositions so far to serve their own purposes as to have almost prostrated our independence & national character, while we deprecate their conduct, the measure of regret will be more full than that of reproach for a people who have been thus misled: & I have no doubt that this people possessed of the compleat evidence of their situation will act with propriety—[23]

Several significant conclusions can be drawn from the story of the Pinckney mission to London. Historians have dealt numerous times with the events recounted here, and textbooks of American history continue to repeat their conclusions. In most of these volumes Pinckney's mission to the Court of St. James has been reduced to a paragraph or a couple of sentences. The view presented usually follows the conclusions offered primarily in the works of Samuel Flagg Bemis in *Jay's Treaty* and *Pinckney's Treaty* and in "The London Mission of Thomas Pinckney," *American Historical Review*, XXVIII (January, 1923).

Bemis' conclusions on the mission are: Pinckney's selection as the diplomat to St. James was motivated primarily by followers of Hamilton devoted to the British interest and Pinckney was subservient to British desires;[24] the London mission failed to liberate American commerce from British restrictions placed on its free movement;[25] Pinckney's efforts concerning impressment were mildly successful and amounted to the greatest success of the mission;[26] and Pinckney was not favorably disposed to the Jay Treaty.[27] In short, Pinckney was a great success in Spain but a miserable failure in Britain.

The charge that Pinckney was pro-British is by no means new; it originated in the partisanship of the times and in the ambitions of John Adams, who had desperately wanted the post Pinckney received. Writing to a friend in 1792, while Pinckney's selection was being discussed, Adams said,

The Duke of Leeds, once enquired of me very kindly, after his classmates at Westminister School, the two Mr. Pinckneys, which induces me to conclude, that our new Ambassador has many powerful old friends in England. Whether this is a recommendation of him for the office or not, I have other reasons to believe that his family have had their eyes fixed upon the embassy to St. James's, for many years . . . knowing as I do the long intrigue, and suspecting as I do, much British influence in the appointment, were I in any executive department, I should take the liberty to keep a vigilant eye upon them.28

This suspicion has hung over Pinckney ever since. To it Bemis adds Hammond's description of Pinckney to Lord Grenville in which he suggested that Pinckney was an amiable person, a description that has helped maintain the impression that Pinckney was subservient to British interests.29 As this work has shown, there is no shred of evidence from any available source to substantiate such a conclusion. In fact, all evidence points to Pinckney's loyalty to American interests. Far from being pro-British, Pinckney constituted a thorn in Grenville's side and, by his firm stand for principle, forced the crisis which culminated in the Jay negotiations.

Bemis says that Pinckney's efforts on behalf of American ship and cargo seizures were "soon absorbed by the Hammond–Jefferson negotiations in the United States and [do] not appear to have been touched by Pinckney at London."30 This conclusion is largely responsible for the general attitude that Pinckney did not fight vigorously for neutral rights, for the idea that the seizure of ships and cargoes for condemnation constituted an unfriendly act, and for satisfaction for such actions to be forthcoming in the legal process of the London Admiralty Courts and the Court of Appeals. Among other things, such a conclusion overlooks the early decision Pinckney obtained in the Admiralty Courts on neutral rights. It fails to comprehend

Pinckney's and Bayard's tireless efforts in the "Cockpit" where legal cases were decided and where the American stand on neutral rights was, at the close of Pinckney's mission, fully vindicated by British judges.

Bemis admits that Pinckney was mildly successful in his efforts against impressment, when, as a matter of fact, he was less successful in this matter than with ship seizures.[31] No permanent arrangement between the two countries was made for handling impressments, although Pinckney was able to procure many releases, particularly in the closing months of his mission. Bemis infers, too, that Pinckney opposed the Jay Treaty.[32] He does this by emphasizing a portion of one of Pinckney's statements to Pickering in which the former denies having participated in actual negotiations between Jay and Grenville and thus disclaims responsibility for the outcome of the Treaty. What Pinckney really was pleading for was a chance to negotiate Article 12 of the Treaty, and in so doing he was trying to persuade his superior that he was unprejudiced in the matter and hence capable of negotiating. Bemis neglects Pinckney's repeated statements favoring the Treaty as the best that could be wrested from Great Britain at the time, and he fails to realize that the Treaty was unpopular in Great Britain as well as in the United States. Finally, Bemis rather abruptly dismisses Pinckney's diplomatic achievements and rests his reputation almost entirely upon the Spanish treaty bearing his name, leaving the impression that the London mission was a failure.[33]

This study of Pinckney's London Mission reaches different conclusions. If Pinckney made relatively little progress in commercial treaty negotiations with the British Government, he instituted a functioning consular system, the first of its kind for the United States. He inaugurated a correspondence with Morris and Short and maintained reports to the various Secretaries of State. He initiated early talks with Lord Grenville on the subjects of impressment and permanent commercial arrangements between the two countries. He led the attempts to free Lafayette. He guided negotiations between Barclay and Humphreys and the Algerians. When Great Britain issued the now-famous additional instructions in June of 1793 and began seizing French goods on neutral ships, Pinckney continually and vigorously protested this violation of American neutral rights. Through his endeavors were revoked the stringent Orders in Council of November 8, 1793, under which all ships bound for France were seized and their cargoes condemned. When Jay was sent to Great Britain to negotiate the commercial arrangements which Pinckney had felt were his own responsibility, he swallowed his injured pride and assisted Jay in every way. For the most part, he gave advice and acted as Jay's sounding board during the negotiations. He then supported the Jay Treaty as the best that could be obtained at the time.

During Pinckney's assignment in Madrid, where he negotiated the treaty which boosted the prestige of the Washington Administration, the British again began seizing French cargoes on American vessels under the terms of the Jay Treaty. William Allen Deas, secretary in charge of American affairs during Pinckney's absence, brought the United States again to the brink of war because of his strongly worded protests to Grenville. News of America's reluctant acceptance of the Jay Treaty eased this last crisis, however, and Pinckney's return to London and his last six months there demonstrated real progress in reaching an understanding between the two nations laying the groundwork for peace until the War of 1812, which finally resolved the issue of impressment.

The period of American history from 1792 through 1796 is extremely complicated. Negotiations between Great Britain and the United States stalled over both sides' failure to uphold the Treaty of Paris signed at the end of the American Revolution. Diplomacy was victimized by inadequate communications. Both nations could do little but carry on, and patience and negotiation proved to be necessary virtues. Although Pinckney and Grenville were often ignorant of developments about which they should have been informed, they did manage, with Jay's help, to arrive at an accommodation. Their joint endeavors and the support and reluctant acquiesence of their Governments preserved peace with honor and introduced to the family of nations a young Republic on an equal footing with its parent, Great Britain, inaugurating one of the great alliances of modern history—one which would survive even the crisis of the War of 1812.

Chapter Notes

Notes to Chapter I

1. Jefferson to Short, 9 November 1791, *The Writings of Thomas Jefferson,* ed. Paul Leicester Ford (New York: G. P. Putnam's Sons, 1895), V, 389 (hereafter, *Jefferson's Writings*).
2. J. G. de Rouhlac Hamilton, "Thomas Pinckney," *Dictionary of American Biography,* ed. Dumas Malone (New York: Charles Scribner's Sons, 1934), XIV, 617 f. *See also, Pinckney Family Papers,* Manuscript Division, Library of Congress (hereafter, *Family Papers*).
3. *Ibid.* For details of Pinckney's service during the American Revolution *see also,* "Letters of Thomas Pinckney, 1775-1780," ed. Jack L. Cross, *South Carolina Historical Magazine,* LVIII (January 1957), 19-23. In the *Family Papers* is a note introducing Thomas Pinckney to Washington dated 9 June 1780.
4. *Washington's Writings, the Writings of George Washington from the Original Manuscript Sources 1745-1799,* ed. John C. Fitzpatrick (Washington: U.S. Government Printing Office, 1931) (hereafter, *Washington's Writings*).
5. *Biographical Directory of the American Congress, 1774-1949,* 81st Congress, 2nd Session, House Document 607 (Washington: U.S. Government Printing Office, 1950), p. 1683 f.
6. Washington to Edward Rutledge, 23 November 1789, *Washington's Writings,* XXX, 465.

7. Charles Cotesworth Pinckney and Edward Rutledge to Washington, 12 June 1791, *Washington Papers,* Manuscript Division, Library of Congress (hereafter, *Washington Papers*).

8. Pinckney to Washington, 29 November 1791, *Washington Papers*. According to the 1790 Census, Pinckney owned one hundred and eighteen slaves. His sister, Harriott Horry owned three hundred and forty. They were among the largest slave owners in St. James Parish. See, "Heads of Families South Carolina, Charleston District, St. James Parish," *U.S. 1st Census 1790* (Washington: U.S. Government Printing Office, 1908).

9. Pinckney to Jefferson, 29 November 1791, *Outgoing Correspondence, Pinckney Mission Letter Books,* South Carolina Historical Society (hereafter, *Letter Books*). All letter press copies of the original mission correspondence are filed chronologically in these four folio volumes in the possession of the South Carolina Historical Society in Charleston, South Carolina.

10. Edward Channing, *History of the United States* (New York: The Macmillan Company, 1917), III, 396-427; IV, 116-124.

11. *Memoirs, Correspondence, & Miscellanies from the Papers of Thomas Jefferson,* ed. Thomas Jefferson Randolph, 2nd. ed. (Boston: Gray and Bowen, 1830), II, 223.

12. Tench Coxe, *An Enquiry into the Principles on Which a Commercial System for the United States of America Should Be Founded; To Which Are Added Some Political Observations Connected with the Subject* (Philadelphia: Robert Aitken, 1787), p. 7 f.

13. Tench Coxe, *A Brief Examination of Lord Sheffield's Observations on the Commerce of the United States of America* (Philadelphia: Carey, Stewart and Co., 1791), pp. 4-12.

14. *Ibid.*

15. John Adams wrote Coxe in 1792, ". . . to me it appears, that the general interest of agriculture in particular, as well as of the nation in general, will be promoted by a discreet and judicious encouragement of manufactures. . . ." John Adams to Tench Coxe, May 1792; reprinted in *The Aurora,* 3 October 1800.

16. Tench Coxe, *An Enquiry into the Principles on Which a Commercial System for the United States of America Should be Founded; . . . ,* p. 44 f.

17. *Ibid.*

18. *Ibid.*, pp. 13-28.
19. *Ibid.*, pp. 87-90.
20. *Ibid.*
21. *Ibid.*, p. 110 f.
22. Jefferson to William Carmichael, 17 March 1791, *United States Ministers Instructions,* Diplomatic and Judicial Section, National Archives (hereafter, *Instructions*). The letters in *Instructions* are arranged chronologically.
23. Jefferson to C. W. F. Dumas, 13 May 1791, *Instructions.*
24. Jefferson to Colonel David Humphreys, 23 June 1791, *Instructions.*
25. Jefferson to William Short, 28 July 1791, *Instructions.*
26. Jefferson to David Humphreys, 23 August 1791, *Instructions.*
27. *Ibid.*
28. James Maury to Jefferson, 14 September 1791, *Consular Despatches, Liverpool,* Diplomatic and Judicial Section, National Archives.
29. "S——te, on the Agency it ought to have in judging of the expediency of sendg M——rs. Abroad." *Washington Papers,* CCLVII, 29 December 1792. Washington's date on this memorandum is evidently in error. Relevant debates in the Senate occurred in December 1791. This is further borne out by Jefferson's appearance before the Committee of Five, appointed at the end of these debates, summarized in the Washington Memorandum.
30. "Memorandum of Communications Made to a Committee of the Senate on the Subject of the Diplomatic Nominations to Paris, London, and The Hague," *The Complete Anas of Thomas Jefferson,* ed. Franklin Sawvel (New York: The Round Table Press, 1903), p. 45 f.
31. Pinckney to Jefferson, 30 November 1791, *Letter Books.*
32. Pinckney to Jefferson, n.d., *Letter Books.* Evidently written in early December. The letter press copy suggests an approximate date of 1 December 1791.
33. Jefferson to Pinckney, 17 January 1792, *The Works of Thomas Jefferson,* ed. Paul Leicester Ford (New York and London: G. P. Putnam's Sons, 1904), VIII, 143 (hereafter, *Jefferson's Works*).
34. *Ibid.*, p. 423 f.
35. *Gazette of the United States & Daily Advertiser,* 4 January 1792.
36. *Ibid.*, 21 January 1792.

37. *Ibid.* Letter dated 28 December 1791.
38. Letter from a Connecticut newspaper dated 18 January 1792; reprinted in *The City Gazette & Daily Advertiser,* 30 January 1792.
39. *Ibid.,* 30 January 1792.

Notes to Chapter II

1. *The Times,* 29 February 1792.
2. *Ibid.,* 17 March 1792.
3. *Ibid.,* 16 March 1792.
4. *Ibid.,* 19 March 1792.
5. *Ibid.,* 23 March 1792.
6. *Ibid.*
7. *Ibid.,* 27 March 1792.
8. *Ibid.*
9. James Maury to Jefferson, 9 April 1792, *Consular Despatches, Liverpool.*
10. *The Times,* 17 March 1792.
11. *Ibid.,* 11 April 1792.
12. Maury to Jefferson, 20 April 1792, *Consular Despatches, Liverpool.*
13. *Gazette of the United States & Daily Advertiser,* 24 May 1792.
14. *Ibid.,* 25 May, 20 June 1792.
15. *The City Gazette & Daily Advertiser,* 21 April 1792.
16. Edward Penman to Pinckney, 9 April 1792, *Family Papers.*
17. David Ramsay to Pinckney, 31 May 1792, *Family Papers.*
18. John Churchman to Pinckney, 9 June 1792, *Family Papers.* Pinckney's draft reply is on the copy of the Churchman letter.
19. Jefferson to Pinckney, 11 June 1792, *Instructions.* (Author's italics.) *See also, Jefferson's Works,* VI, 74-77.
20. *Ibid.* The Consuls were Joshua Johnson, London; James Maury, Liverpool; Elias Vanderhorst, Bristol; Thomas Auldjo, Vice-Consul, Pool; and William Knox, Dublin.
21. *Ibid.,* p. 77.
22. Washington to Thomas Barclay, 11 June 1792, *Washington's Writings,* XXXII, 56.
23. Jefferson to Pinckney, 14 June 1792, *Instructions;* Washington to Jefferson, 15 June 1792, *Washington's Writings,* XXXII, 57.

24. Andrew Clow to Pinckney, 23 June 1792; John Vaughan to Pinckney, 26 June 1792, *Family Papers.*
25. Jefferson to Pinckney, 12 July 1792, *Instructions.*
26. Charles Cotesworth Pinckney to Thomas Pinckney, 1, 14 July 1792, *Family Papers.* William Allen Deas was the second son of John Deas of Charleston. Born in 1764, he attended the Middle Temple in London in the 1780's. He married a daughter of Ralph Izard. Prior to his sailing to Pinckney's assistance he mortally wounded Alexander Inglis in a duel on 30 March 1791. Alfred E. Jones, *American Members of the Inns of Court* (London: The Saint Catherine Press, 1924), p. 57.
27. List of Cabinet members in memorandum in Pinckney's hand, 10 August 1792, *Family Papers.*
28. Pinckney to Morris, 8 and 10 August 1792, *Letter Books.*
29. Short to Pinckney, 17 July 1792, *Family Papers.*
30. *The Times,* 21 July 1792.
31. *Ibid.*
32. *Ibid.*
33. Sir James Bland Burgess (1752-1824) was educated at Westminster School and University College, Oxford. He went to Parliament in 1787 where his part in the trial of Warren Hastings attracted public notice. He supported Wilberforce in his anti-slavery agitations. In 1789 through the Duke of Leeds he was appointed Under-Secretary of Foreign Affairs, the position he occupied at the time of Pinckney's arrival. He retired from that office in 1795 and devoted himself to literary pursuits. *See* George Barnett Smith, "Sir James Bland Burgess," *The Dictionary of National Biography,* ed. Sir Leslie Stephen and Sir Sidney Lee (London: Oxford University Press), III, 305-306, 1921-1922.
34. William Wyndham Grenville (1759-1834), Secretary of State for Foreign Affairs (8 June 1791), was the leader of the war party in the Cabinet. He was educated at Christ Church, Oxford, entered Parliament in 1782. He was Pitt's cousin. In 1789 he was elected Speaker of the House of Commons. *See* George Fisher Russell Barker, "William Wyndham Grenville," *The Dictionary of National Biography,* VIII, 576-581, 1921-1922.
35. Pinckney to Jefferson, 7 August 1792, *Incoming Despatches.*
36. *The Times,* 9 August 1792.
37. *Ibid.,* 10 August 1792.

38. Morris to Pinckney, 13 August 1792, *Family Papers.*
39. Jefferson to Morris, 16 June 1792, *Instructions.*
40. Morris to Jefferson, 10, 17 June 1792, *Diplomatic Despatches, France,* Volume 3-A (duplicates), 10 June 1792–19 October 1793, Diplomatic and Judicial Section, National Archives (hereafter, *Despatches, France*).
41. Morris to Pinckney, 13 August 1792, *Family Papers.*
42. *The Times,* 16 August 1792.
43. *Ibid.,* 24 August 1792.
44. James Maury to Pinckney, 25 August 1792, *Consular Despatches.*
45. Pinckney to Morris, 28 August 1792, *Letter Books.* In August Pinckney filed his first note of protest with Lord Grenville, the first of some sixty which were to be filed by him and his secretary in opposition to British actions. Pinckney's first objection, like his last, concerned impressment procedures. Correspondence between Thomas Pinckney, William A. Deas and Lord Grenville, 1792-1796, *Rufus King Papers,* XLIX, L, New York Historical Society (hereafter, *Rufus King Papers*).

Notes to Chapter III

1. Pinckney to Jefferson, 29 August 1792, *Incoming Despatches.*
2. *Ibid.*
3. Certificate of Identification, 28 August 1792, *Family Papers.*
4. *Ibid.,* Morris to Pinckney, 30 August 1792.
5. *Ibid.,* Short to Pinckney, 7 September 1792.
6. *Ibid.,* Pinckney to Short, 11 September 1792.
7. *Ibid.*
8. Pinckney to Short, 21 September 1792, *Letter Books.*
9. Short to Pinckney, 25 September 1792, *Family Papers.*
10. *Ibid.,* Short to Pinckney, 2 October 1792.
11. Pinckney to Jefferson, 2 October 1792, *Incoming Despatches.*
12. Knox to Pinckney, 10 July 1792; Benjamin Workman to Pinckney, 28 August 1792, *Family Papers.*
13. *Ibid.,* James Poyas to Pinckney, 28 September 1792; Pinckney to Monsieur Anjot, 3 September 1792, *Letter Books.*
14. H. J. Egerton to Pinckney, 25 September 1792, *Family Papers.* Pinckney to Jefferson, 8 September 1792, *Incoming Despatches.*
15. Elizabeth Pinckney to Mrs. Motte, 3 October 1792, *Family Papers.*

16. Pinckney to Morris, 4 October 1792, *Letter Books.*
17. Charles Cotesworth Pinckney to Pinckney, 28 July, 14 September 1792, *Family Papers.*
18. *Ibid.*
19. Pinckney to Jefferson, 13 December 1792, *Incoming Despatches.*
20. *Ibid.*
21. *The Times,* 28 September 1792.
22. Pinckney to Jefferson, 19 September 1792, *Incoming Despatches.*
23. *The Times,* 28 September 1792.
24. Morris to Pinckney, 5 November 1792, *Family Papers.*
25. *Ibid.,* 26 November 1792.
26. *The Times,* 30 November 1792.
27. Pinckney to Morris, 30 November 1792, *Letter Books.*
28. Morris to Pinckney, 3 December 1792, *Family Papers.*
29. Pinckney to Jefferson, 13 December 1792, *Incoming Despatches.*
30. *Ibid.,* 14 December 1792.
31. Pinckney to Captain Dowse, 29 December 1792, *Letter Books.*
32. *Ibid.,* Pinckney to Lord Grenville, 31 December 1792.
33. Pinckney to Grenville, 5 December 1792, *Letter Books. See also,* note of 5 December 1792, *Rufus King Papers.*
34. Washington to Jefferson, 29 November 1792, *Washington's Writings,* XXXII, 242.
35. Short to Pinckney, 3, 14 December 1792, *Family Papers.* Short planned to journey by way of Paris.
36. Pinckney to Jefferson, 13 December 1792, *Incoming Despatches.*
37. *Ibid.,* 5 October 1792.
38. *Ibid.*
39. Jefferson to Pinckney, 6 November 1792, *Instructions.*
40. *The Times,* 3 October 1792.
41. *Ibid.,* 17 October 1792.
42. *Ibid.*
43. Maury to Jefferson, 1 December 1792, *Consular Despatches, Liverpool.*

Notes to Chapter IV

1. *The Times,* 1 January 1793.
2. *Ibid.*
3. *Ibid.,* 4 January 1793.

4. *Ibid.*, 1 January 1793.
5. Pinckney to Jefferson, 3 January 1793, *Incoming Despatches.*
6. *Ibid.*
7. *The Times,* 5 January 1793.
8. Maury to Pinckney, 26, 31 January 1793, *Consular Despatches, Liverpool. See also,* note from Pinckney to Maury, 28 January 1793, *Letter Books.* In this note Pinckney assured Maury that he was immediately bringing the case before Lord Grenville.
9. Pencil notes of reply from Pinckney on letter from Joseph Smith to Pinckney, 30 January 1793, *Family Papers.*
10. *Ibid.*
11. Pinckney to Jefferson, 30 January 1793, *Incoming Despatches.* (Author's italics.)
12. *Ibid.*
13. Pinckney to Mr. Auldys, 31 January 1793, *Letter Books.*
14. *The Times,* 1 February 1793.
15. *Ibid.*, 5 February 1793.
16. *Ibid.*, 6 February 1793.
17. Pinckney to Jefferson, 5 February 1793, *Incoming Despatches.* (Author's italics.)
18. Pinckney to Bonner, 5 February 1793, *Letter Books.*
19. Lloyd to Pinckney, 6 February 1793, *Family Papers.*
20. Maury to Pinckney, 6 February 1793, *Consular Despatches, Liverpool.*
21. *Ibid.*, 12 February 1793.
22. *Ibid.*, 17 February 1793.
23. Samuel Ward to Pinckney, 6 February 1793, *Family Papers.*
24. Pinckney to Morris, 12 February 1793, *Letter Books.*
25. Morris to Pinckney, 11 March 1793, *Family Papers.*
26. Pinckney to Joshua Johnson, Pinckney to Maury, 13 March 1793, *Letter Books.*
27. *The Times,* 8 February 1793.
28. *Ibid.*
29. *Ibid.*, 9 February 1793.
30. William Vaughan to Pinckney, 12 February 1793, *Family Papers.* Vaughan was an advocate of free trade. In 1788 he published *New and Old Principles of Trade Compared: or a Treatise on the Principle of Commerce Between Nations; with an Appendix.*
31. *The Times,* 22 February 1793.

32. *Ibid.,* 23 February 1793.
33. Thomas Young to Pinckney, 14 February 1793, *Family Papers.*
34. Morris to Jefferson, February 1793, *Diplomatic Despatches, France.*
35. Maury to Pinckney, 18 February 1793, *Consular Despatches, Liverpool.*
36. Pinckney to Jefferson, 3 January 1793, *Incoming Despatches.*
37. Maury to Pinckney, 20 February 1793, *Consular Despatches, Liverpool.*
38. *Ibid.,* 23 February 1793.
39. Phineas Bond to Pinckney, 22 February 1793, *Family Papers.*
40. Pinckney to Bond, 24 February 1793, *Letter Books.*
41. Pinckney to Jefferson, 13 March 1793, *Incoming Despatches.*
42. Maury to Pinckney, 24 March 1793, *Consular Despatches, Liverpool.*
43. R. H. Davis to Pinckney, 18 February 1793, *Family Papers.*
44. Pinckney to Smith, 19 February 1793, *Letter Books.*
45. Robert Christie to Joshua Johnson, 25 March 1793; Peter Sharp to Pinckney, 23 March 1793, *Family Papers.*
46. Pinckney to Ramsey Williamson & Company, Pinckney to Messrs. Willink & Company, 19 February 1793, *Letter Books.*
47. *Ibid.,* Pinckney to Morris, 28 February 1793.
48. E. De Bays to Edward Dowse, Dowse to Pinckney, 27 February 1793, *Family Papers.*
49. *Ibid.,* Morris to Pinckney, 28 February 1793.
50. *Ibid.,* 2 March 1793.
51. *Ibid.*
52. *The Times,* 10 March 1793.
53. *Ibid.,* 5 March 1793.
54. *Ibid.,* 12 March 1793.
55. Pinckney to Jefferson, 13 March 1793, *Incoming Despatches.*
56. *Gazette of the United States & Daily Advertiser,* 20 March 1793.
57. Benjamin Vaughan to Pinckney, 31 March 1793, *Family Papers.*
58. *Ibid.,* Vaughan to Pinckney, 3 April 1793.

Notes to Chapter V

1. Letter from Bath, 18 February 1793; reprinted in the *City Gazette & Daily Advertiser,* 11 May 1793.

2. *Ibid.,* 6 May 1793; Letter from Falmouth, 15 February 1793.

3. Letter from Boston, 13 March 1793; reprinted in *Gazette of the United States & Daily Advertiser,* 11 May 1793.

4. Letter from Liverpool, 5 March 1793; reprinted in the *City Gazette & Daily Advertiser,* 5 March 1793.

5. *The Times,* 18 April 1793.

6. *Ibid.,* 1 May 1793.

7. Letter from London, 11 March 1793; reprinted in the *Gazette of the United States & Daily Advertiser,* 8 May 1793.

8. *Ibid.,* 1 May 1793; Letter from London, 18 March 1793.

9. Pinckney to Joshua Johnson, 4 April 1793, *Letter Books.*

10. Pinckney to Jefferson, 5 April 1793, *Incoming Despatches.* This part of the letter is in cypher.

11. *Ibid.* Pinckney, writing in official cypher, reported in this letter to the State Department that one regiment was destined to sail from Ireland for service in the West Indies and that more might soon be released for that area owing to the successes of the combined armies in the Netherlands.

12. Mr. Hadfield to Pinckney, 14 April 1793, *Family Papers.* Baron Hawkesbury (1727-1808) was Charles Jenkinson. He attended University College, Oxford, where he graduated in 1752 with an M.A. degree. During the American Revolution he was Secretary of War under Lord North. He served in the House of Commons and was instrumental in framing the Jay Treaty. In 1796 he became Earl of Liverpool. *See* John Andrew Hamilton, "Charles Jenkinson," *The Dictionary of National Biography,* X, 746-747.

13. Letter from London, 12 April 1793; reprinted in the *City Gazette & Daily Advertiser,* 24 June 1793.

14. *Ibid.,* 13 June 1793; Letter from London, 6 April 1793.

15. Pinckney to Jefferson, 10 April 1793, *Incoming Despatches.*

16. Pinckney to Morris, 16 April 1793, *Letter Books.*

17. *Ibid.*

18. Morris to Pinckney, 18 April 1793, *Family Papers.*

19. Jefferson to Pinckney, 20 April 1793, *Instructions.*

20. *The Times,* 4 April 1793.

21. Edward Channing, *A History of the United States* (New York: The Macmillan Company, 1917), IV, 127-133.

22. *City Gazette & Daily Advertiser,* 30 April 1793.

23. Letter from Providence, Rhode Island, 11 April 1793; reprinted

in the *Gazette of the United States & Daily Advertiser,* 20 April 1793.

24. Pinckney to Jefferson, 27 April 1793, *Incoming Despatches.* This part of the letter is in cypher.

25. Crickitt and Townly to Pinckney, 1 May 1793; Robert Forbes to Pinckney, 31 May 1793, *Family Papers.*

26. *The Times,* 7 May 1793.

27. *Ibid.*

28. James Maury to Pinckney, 10, 24 April, 1, 2, 22, 31 May 1793, *Consular Despatches, Liverpool.* Pinckney to Mr. Lemmon, 2 May 1793; Pinckney to Maury, 19 June 1793; Pinckney to Messrs. Willink & Company, 2 July 1793, *Letter Books.*

29. Jefferson to Pinckney, 7 May 1793, *Instructions.*

30. Ramsay Williamson to Pinckney, 3 May 1793, *Family Papers;* Pinckney to Jefferson, 11 May 1793, *Incoming Despatches.*

31. *Ibid.* The date of this order was 14 February 1793, although Pinckney did not procure a copy until early May 1793.

32. Pinckney to James Kennedy, 13 May 1793, *Letter Books.*

33. *The Times,* 17 May 1793.

34. *Ibid.,* 1 June 1793.

35. *Ibid.,* 11 June 1793.

36. Letter, 11 June 1793; reprinted in *The National Gazette & Daily Advertiser,* 13 July 1793.

37. Jefferson to Pinckney, 4 June 1793, *Instructions.* This letter is dated 2 June 1793 in *Jefferson's Works,* VI, 279.

38. Jefferson to Morris, 13 June 1793; Jefferson to Pinckney, 14 June 1793, *Instructions. See also, Jefferson's Works,* VI, 300.

39. Jefferson to Pinckney, 14 June 1793, *Instructions.*

40. Pinckney to Jefferson, 14 June 1793, *Incoming Despatches.*

41. Mr. Croft to Pinckney, 16, 18 June 1793, *Family Papers.*

42. Note from Pinckney to Lord Grenville, 18 June 1793, *Letter Books.*

43. Mr. Salde to Pinckney, 28 June 1793, *Family Papers.*

44. Letter from London, 24 June 1793; reprinted in the *City Gazette & Daily Advertiser,* 26 July 1793.

45. *Ibid.*

46. *Ibid.*

47. Pinckney to Jefferson, 5 July 1793, *Incoming Despatches.*

48. Jefferson to Pinckney, 26 June 1793, *Instructions.*

49. James Maury to Pinckney, 2 July 1793, *Consular Despatches, Liverpool.*

50. Pinckney to Lord Grenville, 2 July 1793; Pinckney to Maury, 4 July 1793, *Letter Books;* Maury to Pinckney, 8 July 1793, *Consular Despatches, Liverpool. See also,* notes from Pinckney to Grenville, 8, 21 June, 22 July 1793, *Rufus King Papers.*

51. *The Times,* 1 July 1793.

52. Pinckney's mother died in May 1793 after a lingering illness from cancer of the breast. Pinckney had spent much time searching for a cure for her. At one time he sent special leeches home to Charles Cotesworth in an attempt to help her. W. W. Burrows to Pinckney, 27 May 1793; Charles Cotesworth Pinckney to Pinckney, 17 July 1793, *Family Papers.* For an obituary of Elizabeth Pinckney, *see* the *City Gazette & Daily Advertiser,* 17 July 1793.

53. Pinckney to Madame Lafayette, 12 April 1793; Pinckney to Morris, 26 June 1793; Pinckney to Madame Lafayette, 12, 18 June 1793; Pinckney to Baron Jacobi, 3 September 1793, *Letter Books.*

54. James Marsh to Pinckney, 21 May 1793; Thomas Fuller to Pinckney, 18 May 1793; John Waight to Pinckney, 4 May 1793, *Family Papers.*

55. *Ibid.,* Thomas Lloyd to Pinckney, 20 June 1793.

56. Pinckney to Joshua Johnson, 30 May 1793; Pinckney to Lord Grenville, 8 June 1793; Pinckney to Johnson, 17, 25 June, 22, 27 July 1793, *Letter Books.* Pinckney to Jefferson, 1 August 1793, *Incoming Despatches.*

57. David Ramsay to Pinckney, 1 July 1793, Charles Cotesworth Pinckney Manuscripts, Manuscripts Division, Duke University Library.

58. Bache to Pinckney, 30 June 1793, *Family Papers.*

59. *Ibid.,* Hunter to Pinckney, 5 June 1793.

60. *Ibid.,* William A. Deas to Pinckney, 25 July 1793; Deas to Pinckney, 26 July, 9 August; James Ladson to Pinckney, 27 October 1793; Charles Cotesworth Pinckney to Pinckney, 28 October 1793.

61. *The Times,* 19 July 1793.

62. *Ibid.,* 8 July 1793.

63. *City Gazette & Daily Advertiser,* 15 July 1793.

64. Short to Pinckney, 17 July 1793, *Family Papers.*

65. *The Times,* 20 July 1793.
66. Charles Cotesworth Pinckney to unidentified recipient, 21 July 1793, *Family Papers.*
67. Pinckney to Robert Forbes, 4 June 1793, *Letter Books.*
68. Pinckney to Jefferson, 12 August 1793, *Incoming Despatches.*
69. *Ibid.*
70. Pinckney to Lord Grenville, 13 August 1793, *Family Papers.*
71. *The Times,* 2 August 1793.
72. *The National Gazette & Daily Advertiser,* 14 August 1793.
73. *The Times,* 10 August 1793.
74. *Ibid.,* 14, 20 August 1793. It cited the case of the *Laurens* which which was captured and held for months in France without settlement.
75. Pinckney to Jefferson, 15 August 1793, *Incoming Despatches.* Pinckney transmitted this to the State Department in official cypher.
76. *Ibid.*
77. *Ibid.* This despite the fact that *The Times* had earlier published a report that the Virginia case had been decided in favor of British creditors.

Notes to Chapter VI

1. Jefferson to Morris, 16 August 1793, *Instructions. See also, Jefferson's Works,* VI, 389-390.
2. *Ibid.,* p. 387.
3. Jefferson to Pinckney, 7 September 1793, *Instructions. See also, Jefferson's Works,* VI, 413.
4. *Ibid.,* p. 414.
5. *Ibid.,* pp. 415-416. Jefferson also protested Article 2 which discriminated against U.S. vessels entering blockaded ports. They could be seized as prizes. The ships of Denmark and Sweden, on the other hand, received only a warning on first attempts. In Jefferson's opinion the principle of the most favored nation which the United States had been using toward Great Britain was challenged by this article.
6. Pinckney to Jefferson, 28 August 1793, *Incoming Despatches.* Pinckney forwarded to Lord Grenville at this time a note of protest concerning the seizure of the *Eliza* and two other ships.

Nor did he allow to remain unanswered Grenville's replies claiming that British policy was not damaging U.S. interests. Copies of this correspondence were sent to Jefferson.

7. Pinckney to Morris, 1 September 1793, *Letter Books.*
8. Maury to Pinckney, 2 September 1793, *Consular Despatches, Liverpool.*
9. Benjamin Vaughan to Pinckney, 5 September 1793, *Family Papers.*
10. *Ibid.*, Joseph Fenwicke to Pinckney, 5 September 1793; Vaughan to Pinckney, 9 September 1793.
11. Thomas Pinckney to Jefferson, 25 September 1793, *Incoming Despatches.*
12. *The Times,* 18 September 1793.
13. Jefferson to Pinckney, 11 September 1793, *Instructions.* In this letter Jefferson informed Pinckney that although Phineas Bond, whom Grenville had previously selected to discuss impressment with Pinckney, had arrived in Philadelphia some time before, no word about impressment arrangements had been received from him.
14. *Ibid.*, 14 September 1793.
15. Pinckney to Messrs. Willink & Co., September 1793, *Letter Books.*
16. *Ibid.*
17. Pinckney to Jefferson, 25 September 1793, *Incoming Despatches.*
18. *The Times,* 5 October 1793.
19. Humphreys to Pinckney, 6 October 1793; Short to Pinckney, 12 October 1793; James Simpson to Pinckney, 21 October 1793; Robert Montgomery to Pinckney, 26 October 1793, *Family Papers.*
20. Pinckney to Morris, 8 November 1793; Pinckney to Auldjo, 8 November 1793, *Letter Books.*
21. Anonymous note to Pinckney, 27 November 1793, *Family Papers.*
22. Pinckney to Jefferson, 25 November 1793, *Incoming Despatches.*
23. *Ibid.*
24. *Ibid.* This part of the letter was in cypher.
25. *Ibid.* Also in cypher.
26. *Ibid.* Also in cypher.
27. *Ibid.*, 27 November 1793. Also in cypher.
28. Short to Pinckney, 4 December 1793, *Family Papers.*
29. Pinckney to Jefferson, 17 December 1793, *Incoming Despatches.*

30. Morris to Jefferson, 10 October 1793, *Diplomatic Despatches.*
    Department of State, "Liverpool, September 8, 1790–December
    19, 1800, James Maury," I, Diplomatic and Judicial Section,
    National Archives (hereafter, *Diplomatic Despatches*).
31. Pinckney to Jefferson, 9 October 1793, *Incoming Despatches.*
    Pinckney to Lord Grenville, 24 October 1793, *Letter Books.*
32. *The Times,* 8 October 1793.
33. Pinckney to Jefferson, 26 December 1793, *Incoming Despatches.*
34. *The Times,* 3 January 1794.
35. Pinckney to Jefferson, 28 December 1793, *Incoming Despatches.*
36. *Ibid.,* 2 January 1794.
37. Letter from London, 8 January 1794; reprinted in *The National
    Gazette & Daily Advertiser,* 1 April 1794.
38. Pinckney to Jefferson, 7 January 1794, *Incoming Despatches.*
39. *Ibid.,* 9 January 1794.
40. *Ibid.*
41. *Ibid.*
42. Benjamin Vaughan to Pinckney, 9 January 1794, *Family Papers.*
43. Letter from Falmouth, 8 January 1794; reprinted in the *Gazette
    of the United States & Daily Advertiser,* 12 April 1794.
44. Pinckney to Edmund Randolph, 2 April 1794, *Incoming Des-
    patches.*
45. *Ibid.*
46. Randolph to Pinckney, 8 March 1794, *Instructions.*
47. *Ibid.,* 17 April 1794.

Notes to Chapter VII

1. Alexander Hamilton, *Letters of Pacificus: Written in Justification of the President's Proclamation of Neutrality.* (Philadelphia:
   Samuel H. Smith, 1796), pp. 1-29.
2. *Ibid.,* p. 30 f.
3. Tench Coxe, *A View of the United States of America, in a Series
   of Papers, Written at Various Times Between the Years 1787 and
   1794* (Philadelphia: William Hall, Wrigley & Berriman, 1794),
   p. 289 f.
4. *Ibid.,* p. 500 f.
5. William Loughton Smith, *The Speeches of Mr. Smith, of South
   Carolina, Delivered in the House of Representatives of the*

United States, in January 1794, on the Subject of Certain Commercial Regulations Proposed by Mr. Madison (Philadelphia: Walcott Pamphlets, 1794), XVIII, No. 9.

6. *Ibid.,* p. 55.
7. Randolph to Pinckney, 8 March 1794, *Instructions.*
8. Pinckney to the Secretary of State, 29 January 1794, *Incoming Despatches.*
9. *The Times,* 11 February 1794.
10. Messrs. Crickitt and Townly to Thomas Pinckney, 22 February 1794, *Family Papers.*
11. *The Times,* 1, 15 March 1794.
12. Anonymous letters to Pinckney, 10 March 1794; Short to Pinckney, 12 March 1794, *Family Papers.*
13. Pinckney to Lord Grenville, 17 March 1794, *Letter Books.* See also, note dated March 17, 1794, *Rufus King Papers.*
14. *The National Gazette & Daily Advertiser,* 12 April 1794.
15. Charles Cotesworth Pinckney to Pinckney, 29 March 1794, *Family Papers.*
16. Letter from Fredericksburg, Virginia, 31 March 1794; reprinted in *The National Gazette & Daily Advertiser,* 23 April 1794.
17. *Ibid.*
18. Letter from Boston, 31 March; reprinted in *The National Gazette & Daily Advertiser,* 8 April 1794.
19. *The City Gazette & Daily Advertiser,* 7 April 1794.
20. Jefferson to Monroe, 24 April 1794, *Jefferson's Works,* VIII, 143.
21. *Ibid.,* p. 144.
22. *The National Gazette & Daily Advertiser,* 22 April 1794.
23. *Ibid.*
24. *The Times,* 7 April 1794.
25. P. M. Cornwall to Pinckney, 1 April 1794, *Family Papers.*
26. *The Times,* 26 April 1794.
27. Pinckney to Randolph, 5 May 1794, *Incoming Despatches.*
28. *The Times,* 30 April 1794.
29. Randolph to Morris, 29 April 1794, *Instructions.*
30. Channing, p. 133.
31. *Washington's Writings,* XXXIII, 345. Letter marked secret and confidential from Washington to Jay, 29 April 1794.
32. *The National Gazette & Daily Advertiser,* 1 May 1794.
33. *Ibid.,* 5 May 1794, Letter from Liverpool, 3 March 1794.

34. *Ibid.,* 9 May 1794.
35. Randolph to Pinckney, 10 May 1794, *Instructions.* Randolph acknowledged the receipt of Pinckney's letters written up to 1 May. Thus, ten weeks were required for one-way communication and more than four months for two-way communication.
36. *The National Gazette & Daily Advertiser,* 13 May 1794.

Notes to Chapter VIII

1. Letter from Manchester, 17 May 1794; reprinted in *The National Gazette & Daily Advertiser,* 9 August 1794. Curiously, the editor of the *Gazette* stated after the last sentence of this quotation that "the writer is . . . certainly misinformed."
2. Letter from London, 29 May 1794; reprinted in *The National Gazette & Daily Advertiser,* 11 August 1794.
3. Randolph to Jay, 27 May 1794, *Instructions.* According to Bemis, Pinckney was an enthusiastic supporter of a neutral block against British sea power. In his correspondence, however, there is no evidence of undue preoccupation with the scheme as he merely acted as a relay for the Swedish proposal. Washington and Randolph seriously toyed with the idea, although only as a last resort. As a matter of fact, Britain's rapidly changing policies toward American shipping made the proposal a rather remote possibility. *See* Samuel Flagg Bemis, *Jay's Treaty: A Study in Commerce and Diplomacy* (New York: The Macmillan Company, 1923), pp. 218-231.
4. Charles Cotesworth Pinckney to Thomas Pinckney, 29 May, 18 June 1794, *Family Papers.* In the letter of 18 June, Charles Cotesworth told Pinckney that the invasion of American territory by Colonel Simcoe had united all parties and "revived that military glow which fired our hearts in 1775."
5. *The National Gazette & Daily Advertiser,* 30 May 1794.
6. Randolph to Jay, 8 June 1794, *Instructions.*
7. Pinckney to Lord Grenville, 11 June 1794, *Letter Books.*
8. Pinckney to Randolph, 23 June 1794, *Incoming Despatches.*
9. Pinckney to Jay, 17 June 1794, *Letter Books.*
10. *The Times,* 12, 13 June 1794.
11. William Vaughan to Pinckney, 11 June 1794, *Family Papers.*
12. Letter from London, 19 June 1794; reprinted in *The National Gazette & Daily Advertiser,* 21 August 1794.

13. *Ibid.,* Letter, 25 June, 21 August 1794.
14. Randolph to Jay, 30 July 1794, *Instructions.*
15. Short to Pinckney, 11 June 1794, *Family Papers.*
16. *Ibid.*
17. Article from the *Minerva;* reprinted in *The National Gazette & Daily Advertiser,* 5 August 1794.
18. Stevens Thomson Mason to James Maury, 9 August 1794, *James Maury Deposit,* Manuscripts Division, University Library, University of Virginia.
19. Pinckney to Lord Grenville, 30 June 1794, *Letter Books.* Pinckney reminded Grenville of the delayed response on this case in a a blunt note of 11 August 1794, *Letter Books.* This second note on the *Rambler* resulted in Grenville's advising the American ship's captain to determine what compensation had been granted British ship owners whose vessels had suffered similar fates. It was discovered that although the American merchants had formed a committee to press their cause, no payment had been made. Therefore, Pinckney persisted in requesting Grenville to intercede directly. Pinckney to Grenville, 22 August 1794, *Letter Books. See also,* notes of same dates in the *Rufus King Papers.*
20. Pinckney to Humphreys, 4 July 1794; Pinckney to Short, 4 July 1794, *Letter Books.*
21. *Ibid.,* Pinckney to Lord Grenville, 5 July 1794. His protest served to set them free.
22. *Ibid. See also,* note in *Rufus King Papers.*
23. *Ibid.,* 6 July 1794.
24. Thomas Pinckney to C. C. Pinckney, 8 July 1894, *Family Papers.*
25. Pinckney to Lafayette, 25 July 1794; Pinckney to James Marshall, 14 June 1794; Pinckney to Baron Munchausen, 17 August 1794, *Letter Books.* Randolph to Pinckney, 8 June 1794, *Instructions.* Marshall to Pinckney, 21 June 1794, *Incoming Despatches.* Marshall's mission was falsely interpreted by the British chargé d'affaires in Berlin and by Lord Grenville as connected with the neutral bloc project, according to Bemis, p. 227.
26. Pinckney to Jay, 19 July 1794, 20 July 1794, *Letter Books.*
27. *Ibid.,* Pinckney to Lord Grenville, 21 July 1794. *See also,* note in *Rufus King Papers.*
28. Pinckney to Johnson, 28 July 1794, *Letter Books.*

Chapter Notes

29. *Ibid.*, Pinckney to Short, 29 July 1794; Pinckney to Lord Grenville, 11 August 1794. *See also,* note of same date in the *Rufus King Papers.*
30. Randolph to Jay, 9 July 1794, *Instructions.*
31. *Ibid.*, 10 July 1794.
32. *Ibid.*, 18 August 1794.
33. Letter from West Indies, 18 July 1794; reprinted in *The National Gazette & Daily Advertiser,* 10 September 1794.
34. Letter from London correspondent; reprinted in *The City Gazette & Daily Advertiser,* 10 July 1794.
35. *The National Gazette & Daily Advertiser,* 8 September 1794.
36. Randolph to Humphreys, 25 August 1794; Randolph to Jay, 30 August 1794; Randolph to Pinckney, 3 September 1794; Randolph to Jay, 29 October 1794, *Instructions.*
37. Pinckney to Randolph, 15 September 1794, *Incoming Despatches.*
38. Randolph to Jay, 20 September 1794, *Instructions.*
39. Bemis, p. 251.
40. Randolph to Pinckney, 8 November 1794, *Instructions.*
41. Pinckney to Randolph, 16 November 1794, *Incoming Despatches.*
42. Randolph to Jay, 29 October 1794, *Instructions.*
43. The best description of this debate may be found in Bemis, pp. 252-271 and in Joseph Charles, "The Jay Treaty: The Origins of the American Party System," *The William and Mary Quarterly,* XII (1956), Third Series, 4, 581-630.
44. Jay to Randolph, 19 November 1794, *Diplomatic Despatches, Great Britain, John Jay, 1 May 1794–10 December 1794,* Legal and Judicial Section, National Archives.
45. Bemis, p. 270. *See also,* Bemis, "The London Mission of Thomas Pinckney, 1792–1796," *The American Historical Review,* XXVIII (January 1923), note 25.

Notes to Chapter IX

1. Pinckney to Short, 10 May 1795, *Letter Books.*
2. Pinckney to the Secretary of State, 11 June 1795, *Incoming Despatches.*
3. Pinckney to Monroe, 27 June 1795, *Family Papers.*
4. *Ibid.*, Pinckney to Deas, 8 July 1795.
5. Samuel Flagg Bemis, *Pinckney's Treaty, A Study of America's*

Advantage from Europe's Distress, 1783–1800 (Baltimore: Johns Hopkins Press, 1926), p. 415 f.

6. Deas to Pinckney, 7 August 1795, *Family Papers*. In this coded letter Deas explains his strong language saying that he was instructed "to press upon the Ministry here the necessity of immediately issuing the orders restraining these proceedings without the ratifications of the Treaty. After these several letters to Lord Grenville I have obtained for answer that he will transmit to their Minister in America such instructions as appear necessary on the occasion." These instructions were to stop West Indian ship seizures, but shortly thereafter seizures in European waters recommenced.

7. Samuel Bayard to the Secretary of State, 16 May 1795, *British Spoliation, S(amuel) Bayard, 1794–1797*, I, Diplomatic and Judicial Section, National Archives (hereafter, *British Spoliations*).

8. *Ibid.*, Crickitt & Townly to S. Bayard, 27 May 1795; S. Bayard to Secretary of State, 29 May 1795.

9. The British justified these new seizures upon their age-old contention that they possessed the right to confiscate enemy property in neutral bottoms—a principle which was recognized in the Jay Treaty. *See* Josiah Turner Newcomb, "New Lights on Jay's Treaty," *American Journal of International Law*, XXVIII (October 1934), 685-692.

10. Bayard to Secretary of State, 12 June 1795; Bayard to Secretary of State, 18 June 1795; Bayard to Secretary of State, 27 June 1795, *British Spoliations*.

11. Deas to Grenville, 5 June 1795, *Letter Books*. Deas to Pinckney, 9 June 1795, *Family Papers*.

12. Deas to Lord Grenville, 18 June 1795, *Letter Books*. *See also,* copy of note in *Rufus King Papers*.

13. Deas to Secretary of State, 2 July 1795, *Letter Books*.

14. *Ibid.*, Deas to Grenville, 6 July 1795. *See also, Rufus King Papers*.

15. *Ibid.*, 14 July 1795.

16. *Ibid.*, 19 July 1795.

17. *Ibid.*, 27 July 1795.

18. *Ibid.*

19. *Ibid.*

20. *Ibid.*, 4 August 1795.

21. *Ibid.*, 9 September 1795.

22. *Ibid.,* 13 September 1795.
23. Pickering to Pinckney, 25 August 1795, *Family Papers.*
24. Deas to Pinckney, 18, 20, 25 August 1795, *Letter Books.*
25. Pickering to Deas, 25 August 1795, *Instructions.*
26. Deas to Pinckney, 15 September 1795, *Letter Books.*
27. *Ibid.,* Deas to Secretary of State, 15 September 1795. Here Deas described the return of Huger and Bollman, two Americans captured in their attempt to assist Lafayette escape.
28. Pinckney to Washington, 10 October 1795, *Washington Papers.*
29. Washington to Pinckney, 22 May 1796, *Family Papers.* Also cited in Joseph Charles, pp. 581-630.
30. Charles, pp. 581-630. This article describes the very important role of United States discussions on the Jay Treaty. *See also,* Seth Thomas Mason to James Maury, 10 December 1795, *James Maury Deposit.*
31. Pierce Butler to Pinckney, 8 July 1795, *Family Papers.*
32. Bayard to Secretary of State, 29 July 1795, *British Spoliations.*
33. *Ibid.,* 29 July 1795.
34. *Ibid.,* Bayard to Thomas Fitzsimmons, 2 October 1795.
35. *Ibid.,* Bayard to Secretary of State, 29 December 1795.
36. Pinckney to Secretary of State, 18 December 1795, *Incoming Despatches.*
37. Pickering to Monroe, 12 September 1795, *Instructions.*
38. Bayard to Secretary of State, 18 January 1796, *British Spoliations.*
39. Bird, Savage and Bird to Pinckney, 15 January 1796; Lloyd to Pinckney, 21 January 1796, *Family Papers.*
40. Bayard to Pinckney, 23 January 1796, *Family Papers.*
41. Pinckney to Secretary of State, 26 February 1796, *Incoming Despatches.*
42. Bayard to Pinckney, 14 March 1796, *British Spoliations.*
43. Bayard to Pinckney, 15 March 1796, *British Spoliations.*
44. Bayard to Secretary of State, 21 May 1796, *British Spoliations.*

Notes to Chapter X

1. Pinckney to Jefferson, n.d., *Letter Books.*
2. *Ibid.,* Pinckney to Secretary of State, 14 March 1793.

3. Timothy Pickering to Pinckney, 23 April, 2 May, 1806, *Instructions*. *See also,* John Clopton to James Apperson, 4 April, 1 May 1796, John Clopton to John Dawson, 8 May 1796, *John Clopton Manuscripts,* Manuscripts Division, Duke University Library. According to Clopton, war was used as the major means of frightening congressmen into support of the Administration.

4. Pickering to Pinckney, 17, 23 May 1796, *Instructions.* When news of King's selection became public in May 1796, the reaction to his appointment was rather violent owing to anti-Administration forces who viewed him as an ultra-Federalist like Jay. *The Aurora,* 25 May 1796.

5. *The Aurora,* 1 April 1796.

6. Jefferson to Madison, 1 June 1797, *Jefferson's Writings,* VIII, 297.

7. Washington to Pinckney, 5 March 1796, *Family Papers.* In October 1797 Washington complained bitterly to Pickering that "a kind of fatality seems to have pursued this negotiation and in short *all* our concerns with Spain from the appointment of Mr. Carmichael under the new government as Minister to that country up to the present day." Earlier he complained that no word had been received from Pinckney en route to Madrid. Washington to Pickering, 12 October 1795, *Washington's Writings,* XXXIV, 231, 336.

8. Charles Rutledge to Pinckney, 12 May 1796, *Family Papers.* Pickering to Deas, 9 March 1796, *Instructions.*

9. Series of notes to Lord Grenville, 24 March, 13, 22, 30 April, 14, 19, 22 May, 9, 15, 16, 21, 27 June, 11 July 1796, *Letter Books. See also, Rufus King Papers.*

10. Pickering to Pinckney, 4 June 1796, 8 June 1796, *Instructions.*

11. Pinckney to Pickering, 14 June 1796, *Letter Books.*

12. These pecuniary circumstances helped to persuade Washington and Pickering to permit Pinckney to accept the gifts from the Spanish and British Courts upon his withdrawal from those countries. *Ibid.,* 14 June 1796.

13. Gore to Pinckney, 24 June 1796; Grenville to Pinckney, 29 June 1796, *Family Papers.* Pinckney to Grenville, 26 June 1796, *Letter Books.*

14. Pinckney to Harriott Horry, 28 June 1796; Pinckney to Rufus King, 24, 25, 29 July 1796, *Family Papers.* Pinckney to Rutledge,

4, 28 July 1796; Pinckney to Grenville, 24, 25 July 1796, *Letter Books.*

15. Circular letter, 30 July 1796, *Letter Books.*
16. *Ibid.,* Pinckney to Pickering, 30 July 1796. King's presentation to the Court occurred on 27 and 28 July 1796. Pinckney to Washington, 31 July 1796, *Washington Papers.*
17. An interesting sidelight to these preparations is the list of provisions purchased for the voyage home. These included six sheep, twelve pigs, one sow, twenty-four turkeys, thirty-six geese, seventy-two ducks, one hundred and twenty fowl, two cows in milk, second calves, two bull calves weaned, twenty-dozen eggs, twenty pounds of fresh butter, four half-barrels of flour, one ton of full-grown potatoes, cabbages, onions, carrots, horse radish, parsnips, turnips, Indian corn, oats, two hundred pounds of corned beef and one hundred pounds of baked bread. Pinckney to Mr. Auldjo, 2 September 1796, *Letter Books.*
18. Pinckney found domestic politics in an uproar. As John Marshall described them (in an unpublished letter),

    . . . Our assembly which you know is in session displays its former hostility to federalism. They have once more denied *wisdom* to the Administration of the President & have gone so far as to say in argument that we ought not by any declarations to commit ourselves so as to be bound to support his measures as they respect France. To what has America fallen! . . .

    John Marshall to James Iredell, 15 December 1796, *The Flowers Collection,* Manuscripts Division, Duke University Library.
19. Pinckney to Washington, 10 January, 12 February 1797, *Washington Papers.*
20. Washington to Pinckney, 28 May 1797, *Washington Papers.* Similar sentiments were expressed by Washington to General William Heath on 20 May 1797, *William Heath–Joseph Curtis Manuscripts,* Manuscripts Division, Duke University Library.
21. Charles Cotesworth Pinckney was among those selected in 1797 to go to France on the XYZ Mission. Earlier, when Randolph resigned, Washington asked C. C. Pinckney to succeed him, appealing to Pinckney in these words:

    . . . Equally unnecessary is it to observe to you that the affairs of this country are in a violent paroxysm and that it is the duty of its old and uniformed friends to assist in pilating the vessel, in

which we are all embarked, between the rocks of Scyla and Charibdis; for more pains never were taken I believe, than at this moment to turn in upon one or the other and to embroil us in the disputes of Europe.
Washington to C. C. Pinckney, 24 August 1795, *Washington Papers.*

22. *Ibid.*, Pinckney to Washington, 16 May 1798. The disclosures to which Pinckney refers were obviously those regarding the efforts of French Foreign Minister Tallyrand to force American envoys to France and bribe their way to a settlement between American and France.

23. *Ibid.*

24. Samuel Flagg Bemis, "The London Mission of Thomas Pinckney, 1792–1796," *The American Historical Review*, XXVIII (January 1923), 228-247.

25. *Ibid.*

26. *Ibid.*

27. *Ibid.*

28. Adams' letter, May 1792, reprinted in *The Aurora*, 3 October 1800.

29. Bemis, "The London Mission of Thomas Pinckney, 1792–1796," p. 230.

30. *Ibid.*, p. 231.

31. *Ibid.*, pp. 233-236, 247.

32. *Ibid.*, p. 244.

33. *Ibid.*, p. 247.

Bibliography

A. *Unpublished Material*

British Spoliation, Department of State, "S(amuel) Bayard, 1794–1797," I. Diplomatic and Judicial Section, National Archives.

Charles Cotesworth Pinckney Manuscripts. Manuscripts Division, Duke University Library.

Consular Despatches, Department of State, "Liverpool, September 8, 1790–December 19, 1800, James Maury" I. Diplomatic and Judicial Section, National Archives.

Diplomatic Despatches, France, 3-A (Duplicates), June 10, 1792–October 19, 1793. Diplomatic and Judicial Section, National Archives.

Diplomatic Despatches, Great Britain, John Jay, 1 May 1794–10 December 1794. Legal and Judicial Section, National Archives.

Incoming Despatches, Department of State, "Thomas Pinckney, 7 August 1792–14 March 1796," IV. Diplomatic and Judicial Section, National Archives.

Iredell Papers. Manuscripts Division, Duke University Library.

James Maury Deposit. Manuscripts Division, University Library, University of Virginia.

John Clopton Manuscripts. Manuscripts Division, Duke University Library.

Maury Family Papers. Manuscripts Division, University of Virginia Library.

Pinckney Family Papers. Manuscripts Division, Library of Congress.

Purviance–Courtenay Collection. Manuscripts Division, Duke University Library.

Rufus King Papers. Manuscripts Division, New York State Historical Society, New York, New York.

Thomas Pinckney Letter Books. 4 vols. South Carolina Historical Society, Charleston, South Carolina.

Thomas Pinckney Manuscripts. Manuscripts Division, Duke University Library.

United States Ministers' Instructions, I, II, III. Diplomatic and Judicial Section, National Archives.

Washington Papers. Manuscripts Division, Library of Congress.

William Heath–Joseph Curtis Manuscripts. Manuscripts Division, Duke University Library.

William Short Papers. Manuscripts Division, Library of Congress.

B. *Newspapers*

Gazette of the United States & Daily Advertiser, Philadelphia, 1791–1793.

The National Gazette & Daily Advertiser, Philadelphia, 1793–1794.

The Aurora, Philadelphia, 1792–1795.

The City Gazette & Daily Advertiser, Charleston, South Carolina, 1790–1796.

The Times, London, 1791–1796.

C. *Books*

Bemis, Samuel Flagg. *Jay's Treaty: A Study in Commerce and Diplomacy.* New York: The Macmillan Company, 1923.

———. *Pinckney's Treaty, A Study of America's Advantage from Europe's Distress, 1783–1800.* Baltimore: Johns Hopkins Press, 1926.

Biographical Directory of the American Congress, 1774–1949, Eighty-first Congress, Second Session. House Document 607. Washington, D.C.: U.S. Government Printing Office, 1950.

Channing, Edward. *A History of the United States.* 6 vols. New York: The Macmillan Company, 1917.

Coxe, Tench. *A View of the United States of America.* (A series of

papers, written at various times between the years 1787 and 1794.)
Philadelphia: William Ital and Wrigley & Berriman, 1794.

————. *A Brief Examination of Lord Sheffield's Observations on the Commerce of the United States*. Philadelphia: M. Carey, 1791.

————. *An Enquiry Into the Principles on Which a Commercial System For the United States Of America Should Be Founded; To Which Are Added Some Political Observations Connected With the Subject*. Philadelphia: Robert Aitken, 1787.

Dictionary of American Biography. Ed. Dumas Malone. 20 vols. New York: Charles Scribner's Sons, 1934.

Hamilton, Alexander. *Letters of Pacificus: Written in Justification of the President's Proclamation of Neutrality*. Philadelphia: Samuel H. Smith, 1796.

Jones, E. Alfred. *American Members of the Inns of Court*. London: The Saint Catherine Press, 1924.

Pinckney, Charles Cotesworth. *Life of General Thomas Pinckney*. Boston and New York: Houghton Mifflin and Company, 1895.

Smith, William Loughton. *The Speeches of Mr. Smith of South Carolina, Delivered in the House of Representatives of the United States, in January 1794, On the Subject of Certain Commercial Regulations Proposed by Mr. Madison*. Philadelphia: Wolcott Pamphlets, 1794.

The Complete Anas of Thomas Jefferson. Ed. Franklin B. Sawvel. New York: The Round Table Press, 1903.

The Dictionary of National Biography. Ed. Sir Leslie Stephen and Sir Sidney Lee. III, VIII, X vols. London: Oxford University Press, 1921–1922.

The Writings of Thomas Jefferson. Ed. Paul Leicester Ford. 10 vols. New York: G. Putnam's Sons, 1892–1899.

The Works of Thomas Jefferson. Ed. Paul Leicester Ford. 12 vols. New York: G. Putnam's Sons, 1904.

U.S. 1st Census 1790. Washington: U.S Government Printing Office, 1908.

Vaughan, William. *New and Old Principles of Trade Compared: Or a Treatise on the Principle of Commerce Between Nations: With an Appendix*. London: J. Johnson, 1788.

Washington's Writings, The Writings of George Washington from the Original Manuscript Sources 1745–1799. Ed. John C. Fitzpatrick. 39 vols. Washington: U.S. Government Printing Office, 1931.

D. *Articles*

Bemis, Samuel Flagg. "The London Mission of Thomas Pinckney, 1792–1796." *The American Historical Review,* XXVIII (January 1923), 228-247.

Charles, Joseph. "The Jay Treaty: The Origins of the American Party System." *The William and Mary Quarterly,* XII (1956), Third Series, 4, 581-630.

Cross, Jack L., ed. "Letters of Thomas Pinckney, 1775–1780." *The South Carolina Historical Magazine,* LVIII, 1 (January 1957), 19-23.

Newcomb, Josiah Turner. "New Lights on Jay's Treaty." *American Journal of International Law,* XXVIII (October 1934), 685-692.

Index

Index

Index

War crisis with Britain (American): 81, 85, 98, 102, 106, 107

Washington, George: 3-4, 61, 73, 86, 95, 97, 98, 110, 119, 124, 125, 127

Wayne, Anthony: 105, 109

Wesel: 33

West Indian merchants in England: 82

West Indian Trade: 8-9

Western Posts, retention of: 6, 14, 60, 80, 90

Westminster school: 4

Whiskey Rebellion: 105, 109

Whitehall: 26

William, the: 50

William Penn, the: 106

Windham, Mr.: 25

Workman, Benjamin: 33

XYZ Affair: 127

Yellow fever epidemic: 76, 85, 105

Young, Thomas: 50